Armenian Women
New Visions, New Horizons

D0942950

Armenian Women
New Visions, New Horizons

Papers Presented at the
Third International Conference

of the

Armenian International Women's Association
Yerevan, Armenia
8-11 October 2000

Edited by

Sharyn S. Boornazian   Seda Ebrahimi-Keshishian
Barbara J. Merguerian   Suzanne E. Moranian
Joy Renjillian-Burgy   Shushan Teager

Production Editor
Aram A. Boornazian

AIWA Press
Armenian International Women's Association
Watertown, Massachusetts

United States of America

Cover photographs ©2000 by Aram A. Boornazian,
used with permission.

ISBN: 0-9648787-3-9
Library of Congress Control Number: 2004116581

Contents

FOREWORD

Yerevan, a symbol of the birthplace of all Armenians, was a fitting site to celebrate AIWA's tenth anniversary as well as its third international conference in October 2000. AIWA is the only organization in the world that seeks to unite Armenian women worldwide and to address their concerns and interests. Armenian women from both the diaspora and Armenia came together for three days of meetings covering an extensive range of topics. Women who arrived as strangers and parted as friends found strength and a common purpose through their diversity. Together we charted a course for the future, seeking "New Visions, New Horizons," in an invigorating atmosphere.

AIWA strives to instill in Armenian women the confidence to achieve, to participate fully with their thoughts and actions in society, to engage in all professions, as well as the political process, and to commit to public service. In the face of ignorance and prejudice, the absence of role models, low initiative and insufficient information, AIWA encourages Armenian women to become leading problem-solvers in today's world. We saw in Yerevan that Armenia is a nation struggling to become open and democratic but is oppressed by harsh economic conditions. Women can have a powerful influence in the future of Armenia—an influence that may determine the success of Armenia as a democracy. AIWA, therefore, is publishing the proceedings of this historic conference to preserve the contributions made there and also to extend the international dialogue and understanding of Armenian women's issues.

Building coalitions to help where needed was an important theme of the conference, along with the call to transform cooperative efforts into action. Hardly daunted by the challenges ahead, the participants were energized by their conference experience, recalling the words of the Armenian woman poet, Shushanig Gurghinian, "We are all equal and equal to the fight."

Suzanne E. Moranian, Ph. D., Presiding President

PREFACE

I had the honor of serving as the conference program chair for AIWA's third international conference which was held in Yerevan, Armenia, on October 9 -11, 2000. The conference featured many speakers and topics that were at the core of AIWA's effort to educate Armenian women about many subjects affecting the lives of Armenian women.

This conference was especially significant to me because it took place in our homeland. The opportunity to connect and network with so many educated and talented Armenian women from Armenia was inspiring. I believe this conference allowed the AIWA membership the opportunity to assess firsthand the needs of the women of Armenia and to continue to plan programs devoted to helping and enriching their lives.

The objective of the conference was to offer a rich agenda to empower the present generation of Armenian women. By bringing together a large group of very talented women with expertise in different fields, we were able to have presentations on various topics including health, family issues, history, social issues, education, leadership, arts, literature, and economic security. I was impressed with how the activities of the conference were carried forward with energy and zest, with persistence and care, and with a sense of common purpose.

This conference book represents the compilation of the majority of the papers presented at the conference. It is hoped that this book, as a historical record of the activities of AIWA's third international conference, will inspire the present generation of Armenian women in Armenia and the diaspora to play a crucial role in all spheres of society.

Seda Ebrahimi-Keshishian, Ph. D., Program Chair

Welcoming Statements

Welcome to Armenia

Hranoush Hakobyan

I am honored to welcome the Third Conference of the Armenian International Women's Association to our motherland, the Republic of Armenia.

At the dawn of the third millennium and on the eve of the 1700th anniversary of the adoption of Christianity in Armenia as a state religion, it is noteworthy that my compatriots from different parts of the world, our noble and beautiful women, planned to hold this conference in the Armenian homeland, proudly in view of the biblical Mount Ararat.

I want to thank you for accepting our invitation and supporting us to get together.

Realizing their historic mission, Armenian women cooperate and unite. The phenomenon of an Armenian woman is a subject for a special scientific investigation.

In the course of history Armenian women never lost their confidence. Their vision was full of hope and optimism. They entered the 21st century with expectations of new perspective and horizons.

The beginning of the century was disastrous for Armenia and the Armenian people. The ruthless leaders of Ottoman Turkey organized the genocide of Armenians, which resulted in over 1.5 million Armenian victims. The objective of the Turkish anti-Armenian policy was "… to leave one single Armenian alive for a museum." But their monstrous and inhuman plans failed. Those who survived were dispersed all over the world. Our mothers and fathers, brothers and sisters, having witnessed ravages and bloody massacres and having lost their homeland and relatives, as our poet says, took the crook and knocked about the world. They settled abroad, feeling homesick for their fatherland, and informed the whole world about themselves, about Armenia and Armenian people and about the glorious pages of our centuries-old history. Armenians became good citizens and succeeded both in Armenia and in their host countries. The whole world learned about the great talent of William Saroyan, Charles Aznavour, Victor Hambardzumyan, Martiros Saryan, Hovhannes Baghramyan, Aram Khachaturyan and others. Both in Armenia and in the diaspora the Armenians succeeded in maintaining their language and their identity. Moreover, they united even more closely and created churches, schools and communities.

In addition to struggling for survival, the Armenian people tried to preserve the Armenian culture while living in foreign countries. Today, four generations of Armenians have succeeded in keeping the Armenian spirit alive abroad. And closing the 20th century Armenian women, answering the call of duty, destiny and dignity, established the Armenian International Women's Association to unite Armenian women worldwide.

It is noteworthy, that AIWA's Third International Conference follows the Armenia-Diaspora Congress held a year ago. Our Armenian women's conference is undoubtedly the continuation of the Armenia-Diaspora Congress and realizes the directives issued by the latter.

What are the expectations from this conference? Through the AIWA's Third International Conference we want:

- To report our unity and common interests worldwide.
- To strengthen links between the homeland and diaspora.
- To give fresh impetus to Armenian women in their noble endeavor to keep the Armenian spirit alive.

- To provide excellent opportunities for women who come from different cultures and diverse specialties with the vision to cooperate and act united in the current era of economic globalization and liberalization.

- To open new perspectives and horizons, and give new energy and strength not only to women in Armenia, who carry the heavy burden of transformation, but also to the women worldwide, who share the difficulties and successes of the homeland.

AIWA's Third International Conference is the first large-scale women's conference among those held jointly with the diaspora. I hope the presenters and participants in this conference will have open debates and discussions and make suggestions on strengthening links between homeland and diaspora and solving the current problems by utilizing the great potential and experience of Armenian women. We already have the experience of working together. Alas, we gained that experience during the disastrous earthquake of 1988 while working with churches, political parties in the diaspora, the Armenian General Benevolent Union, the American Assembly of Armenia, the Armenian Relief Society and other organizations.

Twelve years have passed since the earthquake. Regretfully, only minor changes have been recorded in the socio-economic field. Any initiative should be based on the self-evident truth that if there be no homeland there could be no diaspora. What do we have today: regional armed conflicts, a deteriorating economy, worsening social situation, aging society, and mass emigration?

But this is our country and nobody will come and change it. Yes, our country is a nine-year-old child. Yes, we have made a lot of mistakes. But we should join our efforts to reach maturity and correct the mistakes together.

Today, we do not appeal for charity, we do not seek help. We offer cooperation and partnership.

Our women have a great internal potential. Their purposefulness, energy and practicality can work miracles. I'd like to give the following example. Four years ago the American Armenian benefactor, Rita Balian, initiated the establishment of the Armenian-American Mammography University Center in Armenia. The mission of the Mammography Center is to save, prolong and improve the lives of women, hence promoting the physical and psychological well-being of Armenian families. The center provides early diagnosis of breast cancer, as well as treatment in the form of surgery, chemotherapy, radiation, and prostheses. The Mammography Center serves as an educational and scientific center for the students and post-graduates of Yerevan Medical University. Another important point to be noted is the provision of employment for 20 people. The Mammography Center develops day-by-day and new results are obtained due to Rita Balian's devoted work and considerable contribution of her family, as well as the great support of diasporan women and the U.S. government.

We should be able to note and assess our achievements and should not give way to despair. Every Armenian should feel willing to contribute to the revival of our fatherland and to the development and strengthening of Armenian statehood. Each one of us should be a part of Armenia's nation-building process and should make every effort to contribute to the reduction of mass emigration. The main aim of all of us should be to heal the wounds of our bleeding country.

We should learn the lessons of the past to avoid making the same mistakes again. First of all, we should create a good moral and psychological climate both in the homeland and in the diaspora. It is also necessary to create an atmosphere of mutual confidence and respect, and to establish firm collaboration. These will be beneficial and advantageous with economic globalization and the introduction of new information technologies. Women can play a significant role in promoting the spheres of business, education, culture, and health. They can serve in the development of our country by bridging the homeland and the diaspora, and uniting their strengths and possibilities. No nation in the world has so many organizations and institutions across the globe as the Armenians have. The name of each of these organizations begins with or ends in the word "Armenian." Whether political or charitable, whether church or non-governmental, these organizations should be beneficial to our nation. As a non-governmental organization, we can collaborate with the Republic of Armenia government and find solutions to various problems facing us.

Our aims and objectives are:

1. To promote public awareness in Armenia and in the diaspora of the importance of leaving aside personal ambitions and to get rid of the sense of superiority towards each other, cooperating and working together in order to overcome the current economic crisis and make our state and nation even stronger.

2. To keep the Armenian spirit alive. The independent Armenian state and all its sections, as well as all the Armenian institutions in the diaspora, should make every endeavor to preserve the Armenian language and culture in all Armenian communities. The youth should be actively involved in this.

3. To take part in the establishment and strengthening of Armenian statehood. To pursue both the problem of Artsakh and the acknowledgement of Armenian Genocide. To undertake lobbying activities in different countries.

4. To lay a foundation for partnerships with the diaspora in the fields of business, health, education, and culture. To implement consulting, professional, and educational projects.

5. To participate in the implementation of charitable projects helping orphans and disabled people. To start a movement, "In Aid of the Elderly," for providing support to the elderly people living in Armenia by seniors living abroad.

6. To be actively involved in the process of road construction in Armenia initiated and implemented by the "Hayastan" All-Armenia Fund.

7. To promote the Pan-Armenian Games.

8. To suggest that the Ministry of Education work out a general system of teaching the Armenian language, history and traditions in all Armenian communities.

9. To suggest that the Armenian movie studio make films about Armenia.

The airplane has three wheels, and if one of the wheels does not open, God forbid, it will end in a tragedy. The Armenian nation is the like a three-wheeled airplane, its wheels being Armenia, Nagorno Karabagh and the diaspora. In order for the Armenian airplane to fly higher and higher and forever, the three wheels should work together in perfect harmony.

We are a world nation because there are Armenians living in all corners of the world. If information technology is used well, we will be able to take part in discussing and solving the current national issues together.

In the course of history, the role of Armenian women in keeping the family firm, in promoting the nation-building process, in sustaining the nation, in rescuing and strengthening the homeland has been invaluable. We've covered a long and difficult, but interesting, path and still have further to go. Entering the 21st century, we will try to acknowledge our opportunities and possibilities, to assess our accomplishments, to set new goals, and to outline new perspectives and horizons. I am sure that by combining our power and abilities, by working together with unfailing devotion, and by creating the future together, we will be able to change the world in which we live.

Hranoush Hacobyan, Ph. D., earned degrees in mathematics, politics, and law. She is a member of the National Assembly of the Republic of Armenia. Formerly Minister of Social Welfare, she teaches law at Gavar University. Recently, she was elected to the Coordinating Committee on Women's Issues of the Inter-Parliament Union.

AIWA's Role as an NGO at the United Nations

Joan Agajanian Quinn

I represent AIWA, a non-governmental organization at the United Nations. I bring you greetings from the other representatives as well, Joy Renjilian-Burgy and Mary Toumayan. For the last seven years, Mary has selflessly represented AIWA through her service to several NGO executive and general committees. She is in the UN building weekly, if not daily. Mary singlehandly has kept our AIWA name in the forefront. Since I was appointed as an AIWA/UN representative earlier this year by the International Board in Boston, I have joined her at the committee on aging and violence against women. I have looked into how Armenian artists could be influential in our participation.

As UN representatives for AIWA, we want to interact with our counterparts in Armenia as well as those in the diaspora. Although we are all Armenians, we have different lifestyles; we need to be unified in our diversity. We need to be civil, thoughtful and tolerant. Our AIWA mission is to bring together all Armenian women, sharing and being understanding of our *couriginairs*, our sisters.

Joan Agajanian Quinn produces and hosts a cable television talk on arts and entertainment, and she has appeared nationally on *E!*, *Hard Copy*, and *A&E*. She served on the California Arts Council and the Beverly Hills Architectural Commission. She is on the board of the Hollywood Women's Press Club. Joan is a graduate of the University of Southern California.

THE ARMENIAN WOMEN'S MOVEMENT IN PERSPECTIVE

Barbara J. Merguerian, moderator

Is it possible to speak of an "Armenian Women's Movement" in the past or the present, and how can such a movement be described? Although research on this subject remains to be done, an analysis of Armenian history provides numerous instances in which women's rights were advocated, but most of these took place within a larger context of change or reform and cannot strictly speaking be described as a "women's movement."

Seta B. Dadoyan, for example, has traced the origins of feminist thought in Armenia to early Christian sects which were active in the fourth century. Unfortunately we know the beliefs of these sects only through the condemnations of their enemies. The canons of the church council of Gangra anathematized women who refused to live and behave in accordance with the norms set for their status and role in the family and society, and who instead followed rules of their own choice, "dragging" their husbands along. But the evidence indicates that the critique offered by these sectarians went far beyond the position of women and represented a radical rejection of the existing religious and secular order. In the following centuries other sects with comparable beliefs were suppressed. It thus appears that women who violated the accepted norms in society, or those who advocated an independent course for women, were treated as heretics, whether or not their actions or beliefs were based on religion. It also appears that the advocacy of rights for women was put forth as part of a larger scheme of reform, and not as a program dedicated solely to women. (Dadoyan 2003)

Turning to modern times, the Armenians of the late eighteenth and nineteenth centuries were not isolated from the various revolutionary and reform movements that swept across Europe. The rise of Armenian nationalism was reflected, among other ways, in the drive to increase educational opportunities for women as well as men. Whether inspired by contact with Western Europe, or by the example of the American missionaries who established schools for Armenian children throughout the Ottoman Empire, Armenians embarked on organized efforts to educate their youth. For example, the "Patriotic Society of Armenian Women" was established in Istanbul in 1879 in order to promote the education of Armenian girls, and by 1914 it had established 39 schools in the Ottoman capital and in the provinces. Another organization, the "Educational Society of Armenian Women," was established that same year by graduates of the Hripsimiants school for girls; led by the writer Srbuhi Dussap, the organization opened schools, provided support for the education of needy Armenian girls, and trained women teachers for the provinces.

The activities of nineteenth century Armenian women's organizations were not confined to educational activities, however. In Tiflis (Tibilisi), in addition to educational organizations such as the "Tiflis Armenian Women's Charity Society" (1882) and the "Tiflis Society of Armenian Women," groups were established to deal with the adverse impact of the industrial revolution on women. The "Meghu (Bee) Tiflis Society of Armenian Women" came to the conclusion that women workers "are the most dispossessed, plundered and exploited class," and devised programs to supply housing, training, and health care for such women. (United Nations Development Program in Armenia 1999, 16-18)

During the nineteenth century a number of authors and journalists dedicated their work to women's issues. While not constituting a "movement," these writers drew public attention to the needs of women. Elbis Gesaratsian, who started an eight-page monthly newspaper in Istanbul called *Guitar* in 1862, sought to reshape the self-perception of Armenian women; her leading article in the first issue of the paper, titled "To Claim Your Right Is Not an Outrage," argued that women's rights are central to social justice. Serpuhi A. Yeritsian published *Family Almanac* in Tiflis in 1874. Perhaps the most influential of these early newspapers was Marie Beylerian's monthly *Artemis*, published in Cairo beginning in 1901. Her publication, she asserted, "will deal with the aspirations of Armenian women, will try to rectify the injustice to them, to cultivate their intellectual and physical development, and to promote their equality and liberation." No discussion of the Armenian women's movement would be complete without a mention of writers such as Serpuhi Dussap and Zabel Assadur, whose novels focused on the status of women in society. (Zeitlian 2000, 119-124; Kaprielian-Churchill 1995, 94-107)

Women were also active in the several organizations making up the Armenian revolutionary movement in the late nineteenth and early twentieth centuries. Some of these societies specifically advocated rights for women; others called for general reforms in society which would encompass an equal status for women. Perhaps taking their models from Russian revolutionaries, several young Armenian women became involved in these organizations. Maro Vartanian was a leading figure in the group of Armenian students in Geneva who established the Armenian Social-Democratic (Hnchak) party in 1886. Women were prominent in the development of the Armenian Revolutionary Federation and other similar societies. Again, these activities did not constitute a women's movement, but they all contributed to a growing acceptance in progressive circles of Armenian society of an equal role for women, as reflected in the fact that women were given the vote during the first Armenian Republic (1918-1920). (Zeitlian 1992)

There could be no possibility of a women's movement under the Communism that governed Armenia for the following seventy-five years. According to the Marxism espoused by the leaders of the Soviet Union, women's issues cannot be separated from the larger questions of social organization. During those years Armenian women became very well educated; they entered the workforce in large numbers and were provided daycare for their children. However the "glass ceiling" was very real; women rarely advanced to top-level administrative positions and were absent from the political scene. In the 1980s actions were taken to allot women one-third of the seats in political councils, but they rarely appeared in decision-making positions.

What can we say about the women's movement in the Republic of Armenia today? At AIWA's Yerevan conference, an analysis was provided by Lyudmila Harutunyan, Professor of Sociology at Yerevan State University, who characterized the movement in Armenia today as "Eastern feminism" or "state feminism." Under Communism, women were officially granted equal rights, specifically the right to education and to employment. The result was an absence of a feminist movement, because women never had to struggle for their rights. In the late 1980s it was decided to create institutions led by women to solve women's problems, but after four years this process was overtaken by the Karabagh movement. Women then became political activists, playing a major role in the national demonstrations that took place in Yerevan. But with the establishment of an independent Armenian Republic in 1991, women lost everything they had gained. They were told, in effect, "You struggled very well—now go home, your children need you, your husband needs you." Under conditions of democracy, women were the losers. Their national activism was acceptable, but a women's movement was not—even by the women themselves.

According to Professor Harutunyan, although Armenian women today have the vote, politically they are manipulated by men. There is no room in Armenian politics for women; role models are few. Monetary resources are needed in elections, but such resources are concentrated in the hands of men. An independent state and government has been created, but not a new society. Political reform is in its early stages, and large numbers of non-governmental organizations have yet to maximize their effectiveness.

There is today in Armenia pressure to create a civil society, Professor Harutunyan pointed out, but the impetus today is all foreign—from the United States or Europe. Just as Armenians were pushed to socialism by the Soviet state, but socialism never worked, now Armenians are being pushed to create a civic society. But such movements when dictated from the top will not succeed; it is necessary to move from the bottom up. The international stalemate over the status of Karabagh retards reform efforts in Armenia, she concluded.

According to Hranoush Hakobyan, Member of Parliament and former Minister of Social Security in Armenia, "Women are bearing most of the hardship in Armenia, and yet they have also been a source of innovation that has contributed enormously to the transition process." She suggests that "for Armenia, as a country striving to build a stable democratic society with a prospering economy, the elimination of all political, economic, social, and cultural obstacles for women's equal participation in the decision-making process is an urgent priority." (Hakobyan 2000, 11-13) The Constitution of the Republic of Armenia provides equal rights for women, and Armenia's government has ratified the Convention on the Elimination of All Forms of Discrimination Against Women. Little has been done, however, to make these principles a reality.

The question of the position of women in contemporary Armenian society can be viewed from two points of view: moral and practical. From a moral point of view, there can be no democracy and no justice when the fifty percent of the population that is female is excluded from the process. From a practical point of view, faced with a myriad of social, economic, and political problems, Armenia can ill afford to ignore the talents and potential of its women. Given the fact that the existing power structure appears unwilling to address the problem, it falls upon women themselves to make a difference.

Women in Armenia today are very active. There are over fifty women's Non-Governmental Organizations, many of them providing important services to women and to society. Here is the nucleus for a women's movement, if these groups can come together, develop a program of action, and then work together to achieve results. A study of the women's movement in Armenia indicates that women's rights were often part of larger reform movements, and today it appears that the advancement of women must take place within the context of the overall development of a democratic, civil society. On the other hand, the experience of the past indicates that women's rights will not be achieved until and unless women themselves play an important role. Issues facing Armenian women in the diaspora are of a different order, but Armenian women at home and abroad can benefit from mutual support and cooperation. An Armenian women's movement must work on two levels—for general societal reform and for an improvement in the status of women.

Works Cited:

Dadoyan, Seta B. 2005. "Feminism in Armenian History: Origins in Medieval Heresies" in *Armenian Women: New Visions, New Horizons*. Watertown, MA: AIWA Press.

United Nations Development Program in Armenia. 1999. *Women Status Report: Armenia 1999—Impact of Transition*. Yerevan, Armenia.

Zeitlian, Sona. 2000. "Pioneers of Armenian Women's Journalism in the Western Armenian Media," in *Voices of Armenian*

Women. Barbara Merguerian and Joy Renjilian-Burgy, eds. Watertown, MA: AIWA Press.

Kaprielian-Churchill, Isabel. 1995. "Give Me Your Mothers and I'll Give You a Nation," in *Armenian Women in a Changing World*. Barbara J. Merguerian and Doris Jafferian, eds. Watertown, MA: AIWA press.

Zeitlian, Sona. 1992. *The Role of Armenian Women in the Armenian Revolutionary Movement*. Los Angeles: Hraztan Sarkis Zeitlian Publications. In Armenian.

Hakobyan, Hranoush. 2000. "Welcome." *Exploring Gender Issues in the Caucasus*. Pauline M. Hallam and Barbara J. Merguerian, eds. Yerevan, Armenia: Civic Education Project.

Barbara Merguerian, Ph. D., Recently returned from a semester of teaching in the Sociology and International Relations Departments at Yerevan State University. She received her MA and Ph. D. in History from Harvard University. A writer who is active in many organizations, she is the former editor of the *Journal of Armenian Studies* and of the *Armenian Mirror-Spectator*. She is a founder and past-president of AIWA and currently serves as director of the AIWA Information Center and Archives.

Feminism in Armenian History: Origins in Medieval Heresies

Seta B. Dadoyan

The earliest yet most definitive indications of radical changes in the manner in which Armenian women questioned their status and rights in society can be traced back to the fourth century A.D. Yet the context in which this very early feminism was indirectly recorded is the history of medieval Armenian heresies and in particular the Canons of the Council of Gangra (378/9 A.D.) addressed to the Heretics of Sivas. Many of these canons and anathema were indeed addressed to women who contradicted established social norms and as a consequence were treated as religious heretics. At the time, earlier on and later, dissident factions included many women; and to the end of the Middle Ages at least, five major Armenian female leaders of heretics are mentioned. However, instead of raising interest about the beginnings of women's rights movements, these figures and the issues they represented dissolved in the histories of the sects, without ever surfacing in Armenian scholarship. Feminist thought on the lines of dichotomy between "heresy" and "orthodoxy" is still very much the core of the discussion, and the women among the so-called Heretics of Sivas constitute a direct historic case for study and generalization.

The conversion of Armenia to Christianity was a long process. The first three ecumenical councils and the councils of the Armenian Church gradually defined orthodoxy and heresy. As of the early centuries, the so-called "heresies" and the "sects" became the carriers and contexts of social—cultural protest and demands. Dissidents with various exigencies joined them and became integral elements in the social and cultural development of Armenians in the medieval Near East. The Heretics of Sivas were early phenomena, the Paulicians became active in the seventh century, the Tondrakians during the ninth, the sun worshippers or the Arevordik during the eleventh and twelfth. The settling of Monastic movements in Sivas with the assistance of Armenian Bishop Eustathius of the city caused the displeasure of St. Basil, Patriarch of Caesari, and a Council around 378/9 at Gangra, in Pahlagonia. Constant persecutions eventually drove these factions into Greater Armenia and further east.[1]

"No-Boundary" as Philosophical First Principle.

This study proposes the thesis that underlying both the beliefs and careers of this group and medieval Armenian dissidence in general was the ideal of No-Boundary. Applied to society, culture, religious dogma, and man's knowledge of the world, this principle demanded an open universe, society, and culture. The doctrines and the culture of the Heretics of Sivas, as reflected in the 24 canons of the Council of Gangra, present a unique value as the first and most complete record of Armenian dissidence, of which feminism is an integral part.

These "heretics" were anathematized because, as Monastics, they ridiculed the rites and norms of the establishments of society and church. Harshly anathematized were slaves who disobeyed or departed from their masters. The canons condemned women who refused to live and behave in accordance with the

---

[1] Our source is L. Khachikian, *Pokr Hayki Sotsialakan Sharjumneri Patmutyunits – 4rd Dar* [From the History of the Social Movements of Pokr Hayk – 4th Century] (Yerevan, 1951). All reference is made to this text.

norms set for their status and role in the family and society, and who instead followed rules of their own choice. Consequently, anathema was addressed to women who refused to nurse their children and left their homes, because they despised their husbands, "believing themselves superior to them," or because they held different beliefs. Considering the length of hair and style of dress as "rules" set by the church, women who "cut their hair short" and put on "men's clothes," and those who devoted themselves to monastic-communal life, were in turn anathematized. Anathema was also directed to those men who instead of "obeying" their parents followed their wives.

A philosophy of equal rights within the "Open Society" was another major aspect of the dissident thought. It was translated in the slave and peasant uprisings against the feudal aristocracy and church. The authority of the clergy as mediator before God and man was questioned, and all "man-made instruments" for manipulating the ignorant masses rejected. The egalitarian principles of the Mesopotamian monastics had their roots in the slave revolts of the Roman world and early Christianity. But complicated Christological debates were not accessible to and could hardly have concerned these factions. They saw Christ as "man-risen-to-the-divine," based solely on the commandment of love. The "no-boundary" condition between man and God, and man and man in particular, was natural and in this context "man" also meant "woman" too. In other words, as Christians, women were complete human beings with equal rights and privileges.

Armenian Feminism as a "Medieval Heresy."

In the background of the above, it seems that the origins of feminist thought in Armenian social history is found in the philosophical legacy of Armenian dissidence. But, as persecutions intensified against the sects by the establishments, the image of the Holy Virgin-Theotokos or Mother-of-God was encountered by the archetypes of female heretic, social outcast, whore, and sorceress. As a consequence, the image of Armenian woman was suspended between divine and demonic natures, and the woman as an ordinary human individual was obscured. It is in this context that we find the most colorful and bigger-than-life feminine characters in Armenian medieval culture.

The dissidents were held together by an elementary philosophy of equal rights, and women were its most significant beneficiaries. When some women behaved as autonomous and free "equals," their lifestyle was unavoidably classified as "heretical" and identified with religious heresy. This is why the Council of Gangra anathematized them. Four out of the twenty-four canons anathematized women who refused to live and behave in accordance with the norms set for them, and who instead made their own choices, "dragging" their husbands along, who were in turn anathematized. A brief presentation of some of the protagonists of feminine dissidence will give the reader a clearer view of the historic circumstances.

Indeed, it is in the history of the heretics of Sivas that we encounter the first Armenian liberated woman called *Simplica.* She must have been an intellectual, a reformist, and a social activist. She wrote critical epistles to St. Basil of Caesaria, who became her enemy. There is no record about the content of these letters, but her criticism addressed to "corrupt" doctrines and practices of the clergy gained her threats of punishment of Last Judgment by the Patriarch.

The archetype of female "instructor-leader of heresy" or heresiarch was common, too. Women sometimes held the position of teachers among the sects. This figure is first found in the semi-legendary accounts of the origin of the Paulician heresy. In one of the legends concerning the origin of the sect, the founder of the sect was said to be a *"gund"* (bald) woman named *Mare*. Avoiding Byzantine persecution, she is said to have led her followers towards Armenia in the east. Reference to her baldness is very much reminiscent of the female heretics of Sivas who cut their hair short and dressed up like men. We read in Section 153 of the *Armenian Book of Heresies* that this "bald sorceress" rewarded evil deeds and rebuked the good. She preached that women were common [to all], and spoke of other matters by "demonic inspiration." *Kallinike of Samosata* is another and relatively more historic figure. She taught her sons Paul and John the "Manichaeaen heresy" and sent them as missionaries to the province of Armeniakon. *Sheti,* another female heretical leader, appears in Heresy 154 (again about the Paulicians) in the *Armenian Book of Heresies.* She is said to have come from the "Muslim [side]" to Armenia and seduced an Armenian man from Ayrarat to join her. Their union produced the Paulician heresy. The idea that Armenian Paulicianism was seen as a symbiosis of Islam and Christianity is conspicuous here and the cause is a woman.

Hranuysh, Akhni, and *Qamara* are aristocratic ladies in the *History* of Aristakes. They too were involved with Tondrakians as "instructors" and active supporters of their cause. A prince named Vrver joined the ladies and became their "obedient brother." Aristakes relates that they were the closest associates and co-heresiarchs of the great leader of the sect Priest Kunzik (a monk trained in Persian-Majusi doctrines of Aghvank). Aristakes also reports that these aristocratic figures generously provided financial support to the rural communities, donating private lands and villages to those whom he calls "sectarians." Their beliefs, as Aristakes presents them, are almost identical to those of the Eusthatians of Sivas.[2] The villages of Kashe and Aghuso (previously estates of Akhni and Qamara) saw widespread unrest in which women too were actively involved.[3] About fifty years later and in the same locations, large-scale persecutions were carried out against these Tondrakians by

---

[2] See Aristakes Lastivertsi, *Patmutyun* [History], Trans. & Notes by V. Grigorian (Yerevan, 1971), pp. 91-98.
[3] See T. Sahakian, "La Revolte Paysanne en Siwnie au Xe Siecle," *Revue des Etudes Armeniennes, NS,* 1(1964).

Grigor Pahlavuni Magistros (d. 1058/9), then Byzantine- appointed Duke of Mesopotamia.[4] Assisted by informers, he was led to the "dog habitats" (*shnavank*), as he describes them, where he says lived "men clad as priests and multitudes of whorish women."[5]

Finally, witchcraft, use of talismans and potions mixed in food and drink, seem to have been practiced particularly by the women among the Paulicians, Arevordik, Tonrakians, and the Bogomils of the Balkans, as reported by Hovhan Oznetsi, Magistros, Nerses Shnorhali, and others. The archetype of the witch has always been in ancient cultures, but its massive metamorphosis in sectarian history is a different matter and must be studied in the context of feminist thought.[6]

* * * * *

These brief historic facts were unfortunately never brought up and studied academically. The outlook on women's demands for equal status still lingers over the dichotomy between orthodoxy and heresy, i.e., on the wrong side of moral philosophy. These few historic cases are extremely vivid examples in support. The same rigid mentality drove the medieval feminist debate into the circle of religious dissidence and obscured it. As Paulicianism spread throughout the Byzantine Empire, the career of female heresiarchs contributed to the status of women as leaders, but the "heretical" nature of the arena unavoidably restricted the rightful claims to a closed circuit where fewer women were active but the rest of women who were playing important roles within the confines of "orthodoxy" remained without the proper recognition and record. However, himself accused of

---

[4] See Grigor Magistros, "Epistle in reply to the letter of the Tulaylans" in *The Epistles of Grigor Magistros* [Grigor Magistrosi teghtere], Ed, introd, notes by K. Kostaniants (Alexandropol, 1910), pp. 165-68.

[5] G.Magistros, "Letter to the Syrian Catholicos," *Epistles*, pp. 167-68, 162.

[6] See H. Bartikian, "Les (Arevordi Fils du Soleil) en Armenie et Mesopotamie et l'Epitre du Catholicos Nerses le Gracieux," *Revue des Etudes Armeniennes, NS,* V(1968), pp. 271-88.

Tondrakism, major thinker and poet of the tenth century Grigor Narekatsi (d. 1003) filled the gap between divine woman or the Holy Virgin and the demonic heresiarch-sorceress by his lyrical poetry dedicated to the figure of the beautiful and compassionate woman. Yet this artistic leap too was destined to be classified as "unorthodox" and the author accused of heresy. Soon afterwards, as of the twelfth century, women gained a status in popular arts and literature without parallels or a corresponding evolution in the "official" position of the establishments. Whatever the case, the few figures very briefly referred to above still stand as "symptoms" and indications of serious lags in the lived realities of Armenian women and the historic record of their struggle through the ages.

Seta B. Dadoyan is a professor at the American University of Beirut, where she specializes in Near Eastern cultural/political interactions, the history of philosophy, and art history. Her books include *The Fatimid Armenians: Cultural and Political Interaction in the Near East*.

History and Outlook of the Armenian Women's Movement in the Diaspora

Seta Mekhitarian Terzian

In memory of my family and for all those heroes of my youth who taught and inspired me, we are all so deeply grateful to you, Armenians of Armenia, who for years endured so many tragedies and difficulties and today, finally, thanks to your efforts and your sacrifices, this morning we were able to sing "Mer Hyrenik" not as "destitute and unprotected" but as "Free and Independent," and our beloved Tricolor is finally flying proudly around the four corners of the world and even on top of Mt. Ararat. Please accept our deepest gratitude.

Opening remarks given in Armenian

What an awesome and intimidating subject to be covered in 15 minutes. It definitely is difficult to be a woman and it is certainly even harder to be an Armenian woman. We have no handbooks or maps to follow. We are not an organized movement as such and we have no precedents to help us solve the dilemma of women in this world dominated by centuries of male culture. If there is any solace to take, it is that this dilemma is global and we Armenian women are not alone in this struggle.

The story of the Armenian woman in the diaspora starts with the mass emigration of Armenians which started slowly with the massacres of 1870, then continued from 1895-1900. The number of immigrants drastically increased after the 1915 Genocide and the fall of the First Republic in 1920.

Groups of immigrants left the Old World with their wives and children believing and dreaming that they would work for a few years, earn enough money and then return home. But due to circumstances—World War I, the Turkish government's continued threats of massacres, and then the Soviet takeover of Armenia with its lack of freedoms—their belief in returning to their beloved homeland remained just a hazy dream. A dream that the diasporan Armenian never really let go of. As the years went on and the massacres intensified, the numbers increased and by the 1920s thousands of Armenians left their wealth and their homes and migrated wherever they could, like the Middle East, Europe, especially Greece and France, then South America and finally the United States. The next mass migrations occurred in the 1950s and 60s with the war in Lebanon and the Nasser regime in Egypt, and the last ten years from Armenia. This expanded to Canada and as far as Australia. But never did the diasporan Armenians forget their brothers and sisters in Armenia. By then Armenia had taken a special sacred place in their lives. There were cultural differences everywhere that Armenians went. In the Middle East assimilation was less likely because of religious differences and the existing freedoms that foreigners enjoyed. Armenians created their own schools, churches, newspapers, and community centers. In Europe and the United States in the early 1920s, Armenians had a more difficult adjustment. They didn't speak the language, they were thrown amidst a new culture, and they had no Armenian churches and schools, no real community life. The melting pot philosophy was prevalent and ethnicity was not accepted. Today it is almost fashionable to be ethnic. In those days discrimination was prevalent, so much so that in certain neighborhoods in the United States, Armenians could not buy homes. The men were given the most menial jobs while Armenian women, who were always sheltered and under the domination of men, had an especially difficult transition. Women struggled to take care of their families and stay as inconspicuous as possible in a society that did not really accept them. Economic conditions were not as prosperous as they are today. Armenian women did not know the language, yet had to interact with the local schools, the local community and bring up children in a foreign world. But there was one thing they enjoyed and appreciated most and that was the freedom that the New World offered. They also realized that with those freedoms came heavy responsibilities, which they accepted gladly and became respected, honorable and successful citizens of their adopted countries.

Historically, Armenian women have always been respected and regarded as strong and compassionate members of the family structure. Culturally all women, Armenian and non-Armenian, are considered to be kinder and more able to deal with children and better equipped to handle charitable work. For centuries women have been channeled into charitable and cultural organizations. As Armenians settled all around the world and became economically more stable, they started organizing charitable, educational, cultural, and political organizations. The women were given the responsibility of running the charitable work while the men controlled the political parties and the churches. Armenian women excelled in charitable and cultural work through several organizations that supported schools, orphanages, hospitals all around the world wherever there was the need.

As soon as young women were of age they were groomed to join the existing charitable organizations, which taught the women how to run meetings, how to organize events, and how to work outside the home. Those organizations, even though they did very commendable work, were still basically auxiliary in nature. Male trustees ran the churches, men ran the political parties and, all in all, the community decision-making duties were the responsibility of the men. Women were advised to stay in the background and attend to family needs and maybe raise funds for churches and organizations and turn them over to the men who made the decisions as to where to allocate those funds.

The fate of the Armenian woman starts from her family upbringing. A woman is first her father's daughter, then she is the wife of a husband, and then she is the mother of her son. She is dominated by the male psyche all her life. Because of economic conditions and because of cultural customs, the male in the family was given priority for an education. This is also common around the world in non-Armenian societies. The common understanding was that the son should be educated because he will be the head of a family, and the daughter is going to be married anyway so why does she need an education. Even when educated, the choice of subjects were always auxiliary—like secretarial, nursing, and other non-professional careers. Nobody in the early twentieth century thought of girls becoming doctors, attorneys, or CEOs of large corporations. This philosophy was more significant in the Armenian community. There is no question that there were exceptions and exceptional Armenian women who stood out. In the literary world there was Zabel Esayan; on stage there were actresses Siranoush, Roubina and Soseh; Mayrig took her part in the revolutionary struggle during the 1st Republic, but generally speaking Armenian women did not reach their potential.

World War II changed the world and changed the woman's role in society. The world became smaller—isolation slowly changed to interdependence. While the men were fighting on the battlefields, the women took over at home and in the business world. This gave them more responsibility, but it also gave them a sense of confidence and independence. When the men returned, their wives were a little different. Armenian women followed this trend with enthusiasm. No longer were Armenian women simply women, they were part of a larger community of women around the world. They got involved in the Armed Forces, in the factories, in the business world, and in the arts. Along with all this came the urge for more education and more recognition of their talents.

Thanks to the changes around them, a reawakening happened in the psyche of the Armenian woman. She realized that she had a lot to offer, that she needed to do more, that she needed to engage and participate in every level of community life. Of course the men resisted at first, but some of the women were tenacious. The feminist movement in United States and Europe allowed Armenian women to feel better about themselves. Now Armenian girls told their parents that they wanted to be considered equal to their brothers and needed the same educational advantages. Armenian women started going to college; they became doctors and attorneys and broke the barriers of discrimination. There is no doubt that the laws in their respective countries and the atmosphere around them helped them forge ahead and accomplish their potential.

It has been a difficult transition for women in the diaspora. The first small steps were taken in the 1960s when a very few women were elected as trustees and as church delegates in the United States. But here I have to interject that even in the US government, women were not elected as Representatives and Senators. The only time women served was when their husbands died in office and they filled their positions for the remaining years. It's amazing to mention that American women didn't vote until 1920, that the first woman Supreme Court Justice was not nominated until 1981, and the most amazing that women in Switzerland were not given the right to vote or elected to federal level positions until 1971. I can go on and on, but today the United States has women governors, Senators, Representatives, and now even a Secretary of State. Women are slowly being accepted as equals, even though there is a long way to go. It is harder for Armenian women to cross those barriers because of background and cultural oppression. Armenian women have become successful in the non-Armenian world as individuals but for some odd reason in their Armenian families or communities they regress to their old submissive selves. It is hard for them to shed that docile Armenian woman persona and image. It's almost like they have split personalities—one for the non-Armenian world and one for the Armenian world. But thanks to pioneer Armenian women activists, slowly but surely Armenian women are now participating more and more in their communities with more responsible positions.

Up to now we have taken a few small steps and today we have to face the future—TOMORROW. What does tomorrow hold for Armenian women in the Diaspora and especially in Armenia? Wondrous things can happen if we just put our minds to it. Three words come to my mind: Education, Determination, and Partnership.

1. Education and with it, self-confidence; you cannot have one without the other. It is essential that we women get the best education we can and then encourage and insist that our daughters get an education. At the same time, we Armenian women have to educate their sons to look at Armenian women as equals and as capable and responsible members of the Armenian world. It is up to Armenian mothers to educate and develop sons who are more sensitive towards women.

    Education gives women self-esteem and self-worth. It opens doors for better economic survival and better career choices. Armenian women have fantastic potential—we cannot let it go to waste. We have to leave a rich legacy to our daughters, and those yet unborn. Our parents had a vision and paved the way for us—now it is our turn and the turn of the women of the twenty-first century to pledge to go forward and achieve what seemed impossible in the 20th century.

2. Then comes the importance of determination, patience, and persistence. At the threshold of the 20th century, or even fifty years ago, we couldn't have this kind of a meeting and discuss women's rights and leadership. I remember 25 years ago during a Mother's Day Celebration, I mentioned in my speech that it was time for the women of the community to do more than take care of the kitchen—that they should participate on all levels—I was almost crucified by the men, and the women just quietly smiled. It is up to us to become masters of our destiny. Nothing will be accomplished if we just talk about dreams and the future philosophically. It is wonderful to dream but dreams are accomplished only when one accepts the responsibility of making those dreams become realities. The choice is ours. I know it will take a lot of work, a lot of patience and determination. We have to be tenacious women, then anything will be possible if we persist and we are committed to success.

3. At last we come to the philosophy of partnership. We are not islands to ourselves and we need partners if we want to win. We must build partnership with the diaspora, partnership with other women, partnership with Armenian and non-Armenian women, and finally partnership with the men in our lives. We love our men and we don't want to work against them, rather we want to work with them. We cannot disregard the fact that men surround us, that half the population of the world is male and governments are mostly run by men. The laws of the countries are written by men, and if we want to succeed we have to lobby them and we have to have the men in our lives work with us, encourage us, and help us achieve our potential.

Armenia is emerging as a new country in the family of nations. The potential is there and every man and woman is needed to make our homeland into a stable, economically prosperous, and independent country. But with independence comes the responsibility of safeguarding those freedoms with dedication and integrity. Women have a lot to offer and have a crucial role to play. The future is in our hands and it's up to us to grab the opportunities open to us and to turn our dreams into reality.

Seta Terzian is a graduate of the Armenian University of Cairo. She is a community activist and has served on executive boards of several charitable and cultural organizations, jointly with the Armenian Renaissance Association and the Armenian Assembly of America. She has initiated a Teacher Assistance Program at the Tumanyan School in Yerevan.

GENOCIDE AND WOMEN

Suzanne E. Moranian, moderator

The Armenian Genocide and American Relief Efforts

Suzanne E. Moranian

The association of Mt. Ararat and Noah, the staunch Christians who were massacred periodically by the Mohammedan Turks, and the Sunday School collections for fifty years for alleviating their miseries, all cumulate to impress the name Armenian on the front of the American mind. – President Herbert Hoover

In 1920, an American peace negotiator declared that it was "no exaggeration to say that the Armenians would have disappeared as a nation" had it not been for the relief efforts initiated by the American missionaries. Starting in 1915, the missionaries witnessed the Armenian Genocide and the efforts of the Turkish government to exterminate all of their Armenian citizens. Numerous missionaries in the field protected countless Armenians and saved their lives, sometimes sacrificing their own. The largest American missionary organization operating in Turkey at that time was the American Board of Commissioners for Foreign Missions, headquartered in Boston. Based on reports it received from its missionaries in the Turkish field, the American Board launched a relief drive that was to break new ground in the history of American philanthropy. The American missionaries were the most critical figures in the relationship between the

United States and the Armenians during the Genocide era. They were unmatched in exerting influence and expertise in the Turkish field and on the American home front, as well as in American policy, intellectual, and cultural circles.

Only several weeks after the Genocide officially commenced, on April 24, 1915, the United States ambassador to Turkey, Henry Morgenthau, urgently cabled Secretary of State William Jennings Bryan that the American mission stations in Turkey were begging for relief funds. "Some say starvation threatens," he warned. "Please help quickly." Bryan immediately forwarded this cable to James Barton, the prominent foreign secretary and missionary statesman of the American Board in Boston. Thus were wedded the United States government and missionaries in Near East pursuits. It was the pressing need for relief that brought piety into overt partnership with the political, and elevated the missionaries to a position of influence in Washington. In only a few years, through sophisticated fund-raising techniques, the American Protestants eventually created a multimillion-dollar business of Near East aid.

Within Anatolia, the missionaries tried to relieve what one American, Dr. Wilfred Post, described from Konia in 1916 as "this constant stream of misery we have before us." Their work fell into four categories: general relief, special relief for those considered only mildly or temporarily destitute, medical work, and most important to the missionaries, orphans. Beyond the interior of wartime Turkey, the missionaries worked in concert with the American consuls. Together they helped over 100,000 surviving Turkish Armenians in Syria and the several hundred thousand more who fled over the frontier to the Russian Caucasus. A confidential 1916 telegram from the American embassy in Constantinople to the State Department reported that in Aleppo, for example, relief work supported 1,350 orphans with food, clothing, bedding, and shelter. However, this served only a portion of the destitute children there. "So insufficient are the funds," read the message, "that many...have only grass to eat, and they are dying of starvation by the hundreds."

In response to the tremendous need for assistance, leading American philanthropists joined the American Board, as well as other mission and religious societies, in founding numerous relief organizations. These included the formation in 1915 of the American Committee for Armenian and Syrian Relief (ACASR), which evolved into the Near East Relief (NER). The U.S. Congress granted the NER a charter in 1919, thereby infusing it with political prestige. Naively, the early relief organizers believed that $100,000 would be an adequate amount. Over the years, the United States government would donate $25 million to the NER in supplies, services, and cash. Herbert Hoover, Franklin D. Roosevelt, and William Howard Taft each served as trustees of the NER. After fifteen years, the NER spent approximately $116 million in assistance. It helped well over one, if not two, million refugees – two-thirds of whom were women and children. More than 132,000 orphans graduated from the Near East Relief orphanage schools. Certainly, because of the missionaries, America had assumed the moral mandate of the Near East. "The Armenians will never forget this debt of gratitude," declared the eminent Armenian, Boghos Nubar, in 1918.

The missionaries managed this feat, unprecedented at the time, by adopting the sophisticated fund-raising and mass marketing techniques of big business. Nothing was left to chance nor to unworldly church volunteers. The relief committee organization reflected the new order in an urban-industrial America. It seized the rhetoric and meaning of system, efficiency, rationalization and bureaucracy. The American missionary leadership turned fund raising into a modern science.

The American public regarded the missionaries as the most trustworthy experts on the Armenian question. The missionaries determined almost everything that the American people knew about the Armenians. They conducted massive national,

state, and local public relations tours. Their in-house publications, systematic appeals to wealthy individuals, community
campaigns, and gifts from churches and Sunday Schools were
critical to their fund raising. Through staged events—including
the popular Golden Rule Sundays, presidential days of remembrance and massive clothing drives—as well as by publishing
books and articles in the general media and mounting advertis-
ing/poster campaigns, the missionaries ran a vast information
network that shaped public opinion, educated the country and
allowed the missionary leadership to serve as close advisors to
those in the government. Held in high esteem in both church
and secular circles, missionaries occupied a uniquely powerful
and prestigious position in the early decades of the twentieth
century.

The aggressive administrator of the relief committee was a
promotional genius named Charles Vickrey. He made sure, for
example, in the fall of 1916, when the proceeds of the much-
anticipated Harvard-Yale football game were to be donated to
Armenian relief, that a carefully designed publicity blitz would
accompany the event. In October 1916 President Wilson had set
aside special days of remembrance for the suffering of the Armenians. However, by early September, the White House had
not yet issued a public proclamation. It was Vickrey who ensured that two missionary leaders, Barton and Samuel Dutton,
went to Washington and delivered to Wilson a prepared proclamation for the president's "convenience."

Vickrey's touch also included the posters disseminated across
America that yearly conveyed new pictures and slogans. Some
of the nation's most renowned artists donated their talents. One
poster, designed after the armistice, showed the unsettled refugees; a picture of desolation was highlighted by the phrase "Hunger Knows No Armistice." Another showed a small child alone
and asleep on the bare ground. The caption read "A Cry in the
Night. Would you pass by? Can you turn away?" Countrywide,

agencies gave advertising space for free on subways, street cars, fences, and in commercial areas.

Between 1915 and 1928, over twenty different American magazines ran hundreds of stories on the Armenians, disseminating information that by the relief committee's design was central to raising money. Many of the writers, and often editors, were missionaries, friends of the missionary interests, or relied on missionary information as sources.

Among the many publications that covered the Armenian story, reinforcing the relief publicity machine, were The New York Times Current History Magazine with thirty five articles; The Missionary Review of the World with eighteen; The Outlook with nineteen; The Survey with twelve; National Geographic with seven; The Independent with nineteen; Contemporary Review with fifteen; The New Republic with thirteen; and The Literary Digest with forty-two. Sample titles include "Armenians Killed with Axes by Turks"; "Rescue of Armenia"; "Armenian Appeal to America for Help"; "Armenia: Worst Sufferer of the War"; and "America's Duty in Turkey."

Major American newspapers gave comprehensive coverage to the Armenian question, also enhancing the relief effort. Because the American missionaries were usually the only Americans living in the Turkish interior, the news reported often originated with them. The New York Times ran 146 pieces in 1915 alone. A sampling of titles from that one year includes "Talaat Bey Declares That There is Room Only for Turks in Turkey;" "Armenian Women Put Up at Auction;" "Armenians Thank Wilson;" "Aid for Armenians Blocked by Turkey;" and "Millions of Armenians Killed Or Are In Exile: Policy of Extermination."

At the same time, the State Department provided crucial information to the missionary leadership, which immediately entered the relief committee publicity machine. It was a twentieth-century public awareness bureaucracy. The system of spreading the information across America worked fast and efficiently. Implementing a professional process, the relief committee got its message out—frequently spread on the front pages of every prominent paper in America within days.

Once the funds and materials were collected, it was the experienced missionaries in the field, familiar with the language and local customs, who organized the relief units to reach the destitute Armenian survivors, mostly women and children. Relief work during the war years especially (1915-1918) would have been impossible without them because Turkey was closed to new missionary workers. After the armistice in November 1918, relief work blossomed out in the open. Indeed, the United States lead the world in a massive outpouring of giving towards the Armenians, spearheaded and delivered by the missionaries, with funds raised through the NER. One American editor wrote in 1930, "the special appeal of the Near East Relief transcended anything in the way of a nationalizing movement of charity and brotherhood that we have ever known."

As the Armenian Patriarch Zaven der Yeghiayan remarked with great emotion to an NER representative in Constantinople, "The Armenians can never forget what the Near East Relief has done for them. The children would all be dead had it not been for you. We owe everything to the Americans."

Suzanne Moranian, Ph. D., is an award-winning historian and noted expert on the Armenian Genocide. She is an author who has lectured widely and has spoken on television and radio on the rôle of the United States and the Armenian Genocide. President of AIWA at the time of this conference, she is a graduate of Wellesley College and the University of Wisconsin-Madison. At the Wellesley College Center for Research on Women, she did a pioneering study on the immigration of Armenian women to New England. She also served as chair of Academic Programs for the Wellesley College Alumnae Association and is on its Board of Directors.

Depiction of Women in Armenian Literature

Irandolina Galstian, moderator

Armenian Women throughout Millennia and on the Eve of the Twenty-first Century

A nation's destiny should be sought in mothers' hands – Garegin Nzhdeh

The history of Armenians, one of the most ancient nations in the world, began at a turbulent crossroad of humanity, where nations with different levels of development clashed—some destroying, others creating culture—thus revealing the nature and character of this or that nation. And in that chaos, in the fifth millennium BC, mighty but kind-hearted and much-loved gods as Aramazd, Vahagn the Dragon Slayer, and our ancestor Haik emerged, who fought against the enemy and dragons only. How beautiful and enchanting the Armenian goddesses were. When describing goddess Anahit, the fifth century chronicler Agatangeghos ("a kind angel" in Greece) quotes King Trdat the Great "The glory and life-nourishing sun of our nation, the idol of all kings. She is the mother of modesty and benefactor of human nature," though in the fifth century Christianity had already been adopted as a state religion.

The golden statue of goddess Anahit, which was a few tons in weight, could be considered one of the wonders in Armenia by world standards. In 34 BC the marvelous temple of goddess Anahit was pillaged and plundered by the soldiers of Mark Anthony and the golden statue was broken into pieces and shared among them. The most wonderful and famous heathen temples in Armenia were built in honor of the goddess Anahit.

Another much-adored goddess was Astghik, the goddess of love and beauty. Following Haik's custom, the nineteenth day of every month was named after the goddess Anahit and the seventh day was named after the goddess Astghik to whom Vardavar (transfiguration day) is devoted.

The worship of our ancestors has undergone considerable changes and has reached us in the form of various traditions. The worship of hearth is the only one still surviving. Nané, daughter of Aramazd, was the goddess of chastity, maternity, as well as the keeper of home and hearth. The fire, the spirit of hearth, the symbol of which was tonir (a large jar set in the earth used as a fireplace), was the center of Armenian family, where the community began.

When Queen Semiramis of Assyria became fascinated by the beauty of King Ara and tried to charm him into submission, King Ara the Beautiful chose to fall in battle, defending the honor of his country and wife, Queen Nvard.

Or remember the duel between Melik of Msra and David of Sassoun in the epic, "David of Sassoun." After three unsuccessful blows by Melik of Msra, it was David's turn to give a hit. Melik's mother and sister fell on their knees pleading David for mercy. Kind-hearted David magnanimously consented to grant the first and the second blows to them. But there was the third blow left and David cut the cruel Melik of Msra to pieces. When David was traitorously murdered, his wife, Hkandut Khanum, learning about the mournful news, hurled herself off the Sassoun fortress. According to various historic sources, many noble women, whose husbands and armies had bravely defended the country and perished heroically in an unequal battle, behaved the same way. If the enemy broke into the fortress, the freedom-loving Armenian women would choose to die rather than be dishonored or live in captivity.

The famous coinage engraved with Tigran the Great's handsome face and unique, magnificent crown on his head, minted during the reign of King Tigran the Great, the King of Kings, was widely known. In 20 BC the Roman invaders, having meanly defeated the army of Tigran the Great, minted new coinages engraved with a kneeling Armenian queen's figure and the words "Defeated Armenia" below. The noble, aristocratic Armenian women, being queens or members of the royal court, were tremendously devoted to their people, and had done much to keep the country's independence, unity and power unshakable. Queen Parandzem, the wife of King Arshak II, was a well-known figure of the century. Having suffered the brutal assassination of her beloved husband, Queen Parandzem heroically resisted the Persians for about 14 months, even causing great losses to them before being martyred (368-369).

The Armenian women were also builders. Queen Mariam, the daughter of King Ashot I and wife of Vasak Gabur of Syuni, supported the construction of St. Karapet and St. Astvatsatsin churches on the island in Lake Sevan (871-874); later St. Peter church was built in Shoghvaga.

Queen Mlke (Tamar) was the wife of King Gagik Artsruni. She was a very beautiful and wise woman. A gospel written in 862 and later stolen was recovered and returned to the monastery of Varag in 922 by the order of Queen Mlke. This ancient Armenian manuscript is considered to be the oldest one with illustrations and accurate chronology. The manuscript is kept in the book depository of the Mkhitarist Order in Venice.

Queen Theodora from the Mamikonyan dynasty was proclaimed Empress of Greece in 830. After her husband's death Queen Theodora took the helm of State, and governed so successfully that she earned the envy of many emperors. She promoted the dissemination of the Christian faith among the Bulgarians, created their alphabet, and translated the Holy Scripture, thus becoming the foundress of Slavonic literature. The Greek Church beatified Queen Theodora upon her death.

Queen Khosrovanuysh was an eighth century musician. She composed an ode called "Surprising to me" in memory of her brother martyred in 737. The ode was included in the *Sharakanots* (the book containing Armenian church psalms and hymns).

The thirteenth century historian Orbelyan wrote about Sahakadukht, the Virgin in Black. She lived isolated in a cavern in Garni canyon and composed spiritual songs, church psalms, poems and taught music to the youth.

Queen Shushan, the wife of Ashot the Great of Syunik, by the permission and promotion of her husband built the majestic monastery complex of Tatev and crosier-like Column of Holy Trinity within 11 years.

Queen Sopi, the wife of King Smbat (the son of King Ashot), promoted the construction of the church and monastery complex of Saint Gregory the Illuminator, which later became an educational center. Simultaneously, she built Gndevank and placed a plaque with the following inscription, "Vayots Dzor was a ring without jewel, I built it and set it on the ring as a jewel;" she also ordered the planting of fruit-bearing trees around the church.

King Gagik Bagratuni, known as Shahnshah (Shah of Shahs) was a magnanimous and gifted person. He contributed greatly to the construction of the city of Ani, while the construction of Katoghiké, according to the famous historian Leo's records, was completed with the patronage of his wife, Queen Katranide. She placed a plaque with her name and the date of construction and added unique ornaments to the beautiful architectural monuments. The church of Gagikashen was built within 14 years and resembled the round church of Zvartnots. A monument to King Gagik holding the model of the church was erected and placed near the church.

King Levon III, called the Bibliophile, was one of the last kings of Cilician Armenia. His wife, Queen Keran, was her husband's soul-mate. She is the only Armenian Queen whose portrait has reached us thanks to the brush of Toros Roslin (1262). Levon III and Keran had thirteen children. The chroniclers claimed that "she is like a newly-planted olive tree in blossom, bright and fertile, making this earthly short life beautiful and perfect." The Queen's son Hetum wrote of his mother that "she had a wonderful soul and a beautiful body." Hetum's wife, Zabel, also promoted the development of Armenian culture.

Then the time of pogroms and exterminations began; the honor of an Armenian woman was obscenely disgraced. In the course of new historic events new names of Armenian girls and women emerged on the historic scene—Gayané, Ruzan, Artsvik and many others, who chose to die the deaths of heroines.

We entered the twentieth century accompanied by tremendous losses and a heavy tragedy. By the order of Turkish Mullahs the Armenian language was strictly forbidden: "seven Armenian words equal one curse in Turkish and require a penalty of five sheep."

Entered the school, caught the teacher,
Woe to us,
Opened her mouth, cut the tongue,
Woe to us,
The desert of Der-Zor is stony,
One can't cross it.
The water of Euphrates is bitter,
One can't drink it.
The water with Armenians' blood
One can't drink it.

The entire Armenian population was either massacred or forced to flee. Very few survived by a miracle and were dispersed all over the world.

Grant, virtuous, I pray to you, grant mercy,
As yourself, from your word, you made a ruling to us, saying:
"Offer this gift to God in name of the great salvation, and you
will be holy,
For I desire mercy, rather than sacrifice".
Now rise again, fumed by the incense of this reminder,
You, Oh God, who possesses all,
All is from you, and glory to you from all, Amen!
(Gregory of Narek, Book of Lamentations, 1001)

During the Genocide Armenian women not only fought against the enemy, but also rescued precious manuscripts, books, and gospels from being ravaged and destroyed during deportations and carnages. Gregory of Narek's Book of Lamentations has been revered throughout the centuries; people considered it to have a wonder-working power and healing strength. Today the treasures of our national culture are kept in the Matenadaran (depository of ancient manuscripts and miniatures).

We are the fourth generation since the Armenian Genocide. What are the missions and priorities of Armenian women in the twenty-first century? Each nation has its secret of longevity. The key to Armenians' legendary endurance is their language and their faith, which should be taught from early childhood, regardless of geographical location or political system.

The Liza Foundation was set up in 1994 in memory of prematurely deceased and very talented Liza Ohanyan. As a mother and the president of the foundation, I organize festivals and promote the talents of gifted boys and girls who perform in Yerevan and various regions of the Republic of Armenia. Halls long closed have been reopened and flooded with light; the concerts have been festive occasions. The Saint Mariam and Saint Eghizabet chapel was built near the village of Arayi in the Aragatsotn region, thanks to the foundation's efforts and contributions made by the Women's Guild of Saint James Armenian Church in Watertown, Massachusetts, and the Guild's head,

Sona Iskandarian. It was a great gift to three villages, especially as it coincided with the celebration of the 1700th anniversary of the adoption of Christianity in Armenia.

It is already three years that, due to Mrs. Eva Medzorian's great work, eighty children and twelve teachers of the school in the village of Arayi receive presents and financial contributions from Boston twice a year.

The Armenian people finally gained their long sought independence. Now we are re-establishing our rights and opening the first page of the chronology of the third millennium.

I close quoting the great Armenian and famous Commander Garegin Nzhdeh again, "Armenian women should be heroes rather than mothers of sorrow." The words of Joan of Arc, "If you are tired, have a rest, but never desert the battle-field; woman's love of country is like a divine fire, full of flame and warmth, and it can wake up the sleeping lion of the people," should always be on our lips.

Irandolina Galstian, Ph.D.,is a lawyer and the Vice-Rector of the Institute of Forensic Studies in Armenia. She also serves as president of the Liza Foundation.

Glorification of the Mother in Armenian Poetry and Music

Suzanna Davtyan

Over the centuries Armenian people have put the most reverent and valued concepts into words using the word "mother": we say, Mother Araks, Mother land, Mother nation, Mother country, Mother tongue, etc. The most precious and sacred things are equated to the concept of mother. A mother, like an idea of homeland and love, has always served as an eternal source of inspiration for poets and musicians. Throughout centuries "Our people have revered mothers and dedicated wonderful poetry and marvelous songs to them. These works of art and music praise a mother's love, tenderness, kindness and express the feelings of sorrow, longing and nostalgia for a mother" (H. Ayvazyan). Every poet has dedicated his heartfelt word to a mother. "… we fully appraise our mothers and our people while getting on in years; the older we become, the more we come to realize the essence and importance of a mother" (S. Kaputikyan). When our mother is at our side we pay less attention to her. When parted from her for a short time or, the most terrible, forever, we feel the vacuum that can be filled only by a mother and by nobody else.

When a mother is with us, "The sun watches us with a caring eye / And the world is sweet and bright … " (N. Zaryan).

"Don't you know the child when motherless is broken hearted and can't feel happy ..." (B. Karapetyan). Poetic lines full of sorrow and longing are created:

I heard a pleasant voice,

I felt it was my aged mother,

A little hope flashed through my mind,

But, alas, it was a dream ...

(S. Shahaziz).

How many generations have sung this song and how many more will sing it?

A great number of songs in different languages, poems, novels, paintings, sculptures have been dedicated to a mother. Many artists, poets and writers in praising the mother of God, reflected their deep feelings for their own mothers.

Ma, Goddess living by our sides,

I wonder why, if you are here,

The men look up to see God there,

And pray to him and blindly praise,

If you are only to be praised.

(A. Saroyan)

Describing the story of Raphael's "Madonna della Sedia", the famous biographer of the Renaissance G. Vasari writes: "One day, walking in the street, Raphael noticed a peasant-woman sitting in a corner and breastfeeding the child. The painter was so much charmed and fascinated by the delightful sight that he decided to immortalize it. Having neither paper nor pencil, he stopped one of the rolling casks, took a piece of coal and quickly made a sketch"; hence the secret of painting's round-form frame as different from the others with square-form or rectangular-form frames.

So, we should worship a mother like we worship God. It is noteworthy that the tenth century mystic poet, Gregory of Narek, in praising the Virgin Mary, expressed his admiration for a woman as ideal, perfect but at the same time a real and earthly creature. He praised her with inspiration and excitement, "with the subtle and luminous colors of Raphael, emotive and cheerful music of Mozart, that if colors [were] used instead of words, i.e., if literature translated into painting, the Madonnas by Raphael will seem dull and colorless…" (V. Gevorgyan).

The stretch of sea-blue eyes
Across the smiling sea of morn
Like two light-gleaming suns;
Shafts of light beam down at dawn.
(Gregory of Narek, "Song of Birth")

Mothers give life, heart, will and soul to nurture their children. It is them, who predestine their future: "Will they carry the world upon their backs or will they climb upon the back of the world …" (P. Sevak), will they share the poet's pain: "My homeland is in misery, To die and not be of use to him, Oh, that is the greatest pain to me …" (P. Duryan), will they leave indelible traces after them building castles and palaces, constructing bridges and arches, making the motherland fertile, will they protect mankind from spiritual starvation leaving everywhere "a scrap of their heart, a light from their eyes, a relic from their soul," will they disseminate terror and horror or kindness and honesty, will patriotism and humanity be the credo of their life, etc.

It is women, particularly mothers, who own the golden key to the peaceful coexistence and prosperity of different countries and to establishing and strengthening our state. Mothers carry great responsibilities and duties. It can be said that the future of the world is in their hands.

Upon our coming into this world, the community passes on to us through mothers the skills and experience accumulated in the course of centuries. And if we gratefully acknowledge the significance and importance of what our mothers and nation have done for us, we would feel obliged to contribute our own share to it. So, mothers sow the seeds of love and respect in the hearts of their children towards their history and culture, help them to assess the reality objectively, and implant a desire and willingness to preserve and add to what they have inherited from their ancestors. Hence, new songs of acknowledgment, appreciation and admiration are born in the hearts of children...

And forever obliged to you,
I shall support you and protect,
I'm so grateful and I'll try
To recompense your kindness
Throughout my life...
(M. Atmachyan).

Or the following marvelous lines by Sylva Kaputikyan:
What in life should be requited?
Never yearned to achieve fame,
But for you, in the twilight of your life
Not to look back with regret,
I'd wish to be a hero, to be Great
To return the years you've sacrificed...

A mother's heart. A mother's heart has been compared with the infinity of space, with the depths of the ocean, with the light and earth that are boundless. A mother's heart has been attached qualities like honesty, purity, sacredness and quietness...

You are peaceful and quiet
Like a white color
You are honest and pure
Like a light of a prayer ...
(A. Parsamyan)

Only with the earth can I compare
The heart of a mother kind and forgiving ...
(Aghavni)

The following lines by Hamo Sahyan can be addressed to all the mothers living in all corners of the world irrespective of their language and nationality and the colour of skin:

You are as limpid as my mother's tears
Diamond drops of a spring rain,

You fall from the eyes of a boundless sky
And the sky perhaps is her face.
You are as sweet as my mother's milk
Emerald waters of our springs,
My mother's resting in this clear earth,
You flow out perhaps from her heart.

Mothers have much in common; they care for their children and share their sadness and joy; they are proud of their children and their success as adults gives them happiness and a sense of fulfillment. That is why the works of art and music praising a mother are full of love and tenderness. Describing his mother, a well-known Armenian poet Gevorg Emin has noticed an interesting trait typical of Armenian mothers:

My mother speaks so quietly,
So modestly, by herself,
If something good, she whispers it
Not to be heard ... by grief again.
Even in times of happiness
She is afraid to rejoice
As if she sins unwittingly
And cannot be absolved from.
I look at her with indignation
But she whispers fearfully:
"Make merry but be careful
Not to ... disturb ... the grief again.
The pain is hard to withstand,
Success is harder to endure,
Don't be angry with me, son,
And don't lead me astray, please."
Oh, I wonder, how the grief
Could frighten my ma since then
She has become humble and meek
For fear of meeting that witch again.
And though the corners of our home

Are settled with joy and happiness,
She still keeps to the lifelong grief
Her thinly veiled faithfulness."

Women may occupy various top positions, receive many awards but the mother's position is the highest one, as every woman longs for the word "mommy" to be heard in her address. So great is the yearning to become a mother that women make every endeavor, make sacrifices, go through sufferings or even undergo surgical operations to have the desire satisfied. Each mother can distinguish the voice calling her among thousands of the others. "Mother is the biggest treasure in this world; lucky is he, who has a mother" (Sarmen). The songs and poems praising a mother's kindness, patience and generosity are numberless.

We can endlessly glorify mothers but as Gregory of Narek says:

… For, even if I make sea water be like ink,
And measure parchment with dimensions of the fields,
Producing writing pens from groves of reeds,
In that case either …
… we'll not be able to describe the whole perfection of a mother. And
… If all cedars of Lebanon could be adjoined,
I would have made of them a single arm of balance,
Placing on one pan of righteousness hitting the highest point
As counterbalance, the Mount Ararat,
In that case either, will the pan of righteousness be never balanced,
Will never hold equal to the pan abundant …
… with mother's love.

A mother is like a candle. It burns to give light and warmth to her children, to her people and to the whole mankind:

My mother is old, my mother is weak,
My mother is a simple woman,

But she's a candle as mighty as the sun
Shining in my motherland ...

Suzanna Davtyan is a sociologist, a doctoral candidate of philosophical sciences, and Associate Professor at Yerevan State Medical University. She has numerous publications on Armenian folklore and popular songs.

Celebrating the Armenian Woman: The Mother in Peter Najarian's Voyages

Arpi Sarafian

I have always associated storytelling with my grandmother and can understand the reason that Peter Najarian[1] would dedicate his 1971 novel, *Voyages*, (second edition, 1979) which in his Preface he describes as "one moment in the many moments we sit together and share our songs and our narratives," to his mother, Zaroohe Najarian.[2] In fact, the dedication paves the way for the crucial role the fictional mother, Melina, plays in helping Najarian tell his story. In an intricate structure of alternating narrators, Melina's voice dominates, giving authority and subjectivity to a female voice.

[1] Peter Najarian is an American writer residing in Berkeley, California. For the most part, Najarian's writing stems from his experiences of growing up in America as the son of immigrants, away from his mother's beloved *aiki* in the old country. The insecurities, the fear and the alienation of life in exile, seeking, and not finding, a home, are central themes in Najarian's writing. My premise for looking at the figure of the mother in Najarian's writing, fiction, more specifically his first novel, the 1971 *Voyages*, is that reading about and interpreting strong and positive female characters in literature can be very effective in empowering women and helping them to deal with issues that concern them in a more focused manner.

[2] It is no coincidence that several notable American-Armenian writers foreground the mother, or the grandmother, in their writing. William Saroyan's grandmother, Lucy Garaoghalanian, a strong, life-loving woman who played a major role in Saroyan's life, appears in several of his stories. A more recent example is Peter Balakian's 1997 memoir, *Black Dog of Fate,* which opens with the description of a photograph of Balakian's grandmother, a courageous woman who connects her grandson to his past and to his people. The Armenian Genocide becomes central to Balakian's poetic imagination.

Voyages is about a people trying to find "a new world in an old world." More specifically, it is about a young man, Aram Tomasian, the son of immigrants, "a man who once lived in another country" (Najarian 1979, p. 57), searching for his identity and a way of living in a country not his own. I argue that (besides Aram's own voice) the mother's voice is best suited to tell the story of her son, who is desperately seeking "a home in America. ...everyone was going to America" (p. 56). Aram is doomed to "wander and search... wander and search" (p. 145). Melina's casual reference, "You were almost born in England, my son" (p. 55), conjures up memories, unspeakable horrors suffered by a people who were uprooted from their ancestral homeland, taken on a death march into the desert and left there to die or, in the case of the very few, to miraculously escape the massacre and wander the world in search of a home.

While set in America in the fifties and the sixties,[3] the novel focuses particularly on the time the little girl was separated from her family, on that "one morning my mother told me not to go near my father and baby brother who were dead together at the side of the road" (Najarian 1979, p. 50). A whole people were washed away in blood. Najarian says, "The men were dead. Or dying. Crippled. Or silent." Few "were left who spoke the same language" (p. 28). The communal bath, where "once women, as in a seraglio, rubbed one another, later sat in burnous towels and gossiped eating grapefruit," was also gone. "Only [Aram] was left to rub her back" (p. 39).

The book opens with Melina in her kitchen stuffing food into jars and rolling "derev dolma" into neat cylinders as she coaxes her son to come to breakfast, to the choreg, the feta cheese

---

[3] Besides being the story of the violence and the terror of history ever present in the psyche of the Armenian people, Najarian's novel is also a strong critique of mainstream American culture, of its focus on conformity and standardization. "Get up! Get up! To the morning commandment: Thou shalt do something" (Najarian 1979, p. 30), best expresses Aram's resentment at a culture that makes it difficult for someone like him, someone who is different, to make it in America.

and wrinkled olives laid on the kitchen table. The protagonist Aram narrates this particular chapter, yet the mother clearly dominates the scene. Through her, a whole lifestyle, a whole culture with its food, history and values, comes to life. For example, despite her son's insistence, Melina refuses to admit that Aram's father was weak, that he had "let her support him." Her irrevocable, "He was your father," (Najarian 1979, p. 7), sums up a tradition of deference and unquestioning loyalty to a husband and a father.

More importantly, Melina's perspective is one we learn to trust. "How did you become different?" (Najarian 1979, p. 24), besides evoking a mother's concern (so unique in its intensity and urgency) for the well-being of her son, captures the pathology of Aram's conflicted personality and his inability to yield to the values of "the new world" into which he was born (p. 13). "America asked too much of me and I wanted to escape her, as an orphan from an orphanage," (p. 22), Aram confides. Whether it is the history of the Tomasian family or of the massacres, the mother, with her "multifarious stews" (p. 43), is ever-present. Even Aram's reflections on his intimate relationships with women are addressed to "Ma" (p. 54).

Not surprisingly, Melina survives. The answer to the question pondered throughout the book, could "the strange girl from Adana make a home in America" (Najarian 1979, p. 57) is a resounding "Yes." "Read the writing on my forehead: I survived," says Melina to her son (p. 50). Melina works, marries and, true to the American way, divorces. In fact, transcending the particularities of her individual character, she also becomes the embodiment of a universal voice. "The short and fat illiterate peasant" (p. 8) her son was ashamed of merges with the most beautiful women in art and in life. He "noble and dignified," Melina is at once Picasso's Gertrude Stein (p. 9), and Venus, "naked in her old age on the edge of a bathtub fat and abundant like a Renaissance nude" (p. 39).

Particularly important for our purposes here is the fact that Melina emerges as a very complex character. Besides the "perfect mother" (Najarian 1979, p. 11) to a son who "looked very much like her" (p. 18) and who, in fact, was "an extension of [her]" (p. 79), Melina validates herself as a true historical being with her own lived experiences. Melina's directness and candor in expressing her innermost longings are almost shocking in an Armenian novel. Having heard her tell her own story makes this "wicked woman's" (p. 69) boldness and individuality even more poignant. She confesses, "I slowly awakened to him, to all men... pleasure" (p. 53), she tells her son, as she reflects on her marriage to her second husband, Aram's father. She reminisces, "I was hot under my dress" (p. 59). "Melina the whore's" (p. 60) persistence in indulging in "the first mother's sin" (p. 79) despite the "viper women with forked tongues" (p. 60), and her own knowledge that there was "something sinful in being happy" (p. 62) (she was, after all, the product of her culture) are not typical of Armenian women who are traditionally expected to be holy and passionless. Melina is determined to get her self back (p. 64) after being "buried beneath all those years in her husband's shadow" (p. 62). She declares, "I was free of him... suddenly I was smiling" (p. 71), which shows an audacity rare for any, let alone an Armenian woman.

In a different context, Melina can boldly declare, "I am unhappy," this time despite her culture's edict that a woman has "no right to be unhappy" (Najarian 1979, p. 61). Indeed, Melina has "discovered a selfishness so ruthless" (p. 64) that she decides to get a divorce, knowing full well she "would be an outcast, a pariah" (p. 65). Melina is both a "whore" and a "saint." Even as she keeps connected with her history and her culture, she celebrates the newfound self. On the one hand, Melina cooks and she is comfortable in her role as mother—cherished values of her culture.[4]

---

[4] Like the mother in Najarian's second novel, the 1983 *Daughters of Memory*, "She is her kitchen" and is "no one if not a mother" (Najarian 1986, p. 40).

On the other hand, she faces challenges empowered by her self-knowledge and freedom. Motherhood is as a model neither proposed, nor rejected. Melina is a unique and complex being, impossible to pigeonhole into fixed models and oppositions.

Melina's growth to self-knowledge and mastery and, generally, the foregrounding of women characters in the novel[5] is indicative of a political vision.[6] Ultimately, what emerges with Melina is a woman who was, like Zaroohe Sourian,[7] "better than her husband" (Najarian 1979, p. 62).

Voyages acquires even more resonance when juxtaposed with Najarian's later migrant story, his 1986 *Daughters of Memory*, where again women, this time older, remember, gossip and comment. Like its predecessor, *Daughters of Memory* captures the

[5] Melina's mother-in-law, Annah Bahjee, and her friends Shamir, Nevart and Zabel are only a few of the women that we encounter in the book. In this context of the foregrounding of the feminine, it is highly significant that Aram's own search for an identity and his final coming to terms with his mother is made possible through his girlfriend Anita: "Suddenly all the love I ever wanted from Anita, from anyone, came out of me for myself" (Najarian 1979, p. 45), confides Aram as he looks at himself in the mirror. While Aram's conflict is partly due to his own personality – he was in fact very different from his older brother Yero, who had no problem being part of the big American family and led the American dream of a wife, two children and a house in the suburbs, Lucky Strikes, a Ford—it is also clearly due to the collective memories of refugees whose "wives [were] raped, their children scattered across the desert, the old man and their mother dead by shock" (p. 48). Aram could not have pleasure with his girlfriend Anita because of his memory that Shamir was raped by a Turk (p. 26), and "because when she was a small girl in Urfa twenty Turks [raped] [Miss Berberian] crazy, ripped her inside out, and left her gagged with semen" (p. 131).

[6] The author's primary concern is to create. Najarian is a "young man in love with language" (Author's Preface) experimenting with the art of telling a story. Much to his credit, his narrative strategy (of using Melina's voice) seems to come right out of the fabric of his artistic creation, in no way artificially imposed because of ideological concerns. In celebrating the female voice, however, Najarian validates women—a political statement. I find *Voyages* to be a great work to explore the relations hip between the aesthetic and the political. Indeed, the book evinces that aesthetic concerns and representation need not be exclusive categories.

[7] In the novel, Zaroohe Sourian is the wife of a master musician known for his skill in playing the oud. Ironically, although Zaroohe played "better than her husband," no one knew that "she was playing before she went to school… because it was shameful" (Najarian 1979, p. 62).

trauma of a people haunted by the fear of death, literal death, and the fear of eventual extinction. The mother's plea, "let [my son] do anything he wants as long as he's not a corpse at the side of the road" (Najarian 1986, p. 40), echoes Melina's plea to her son, "Please don't fall down because I won't be able to pick you up" (Najarian 1979, p. 85). Most engaging in the novel are the exchanges between "a bunch of old Armenian women sitting around in a place like Fresno" (Najarian 1986, p. 3) who remember and comment on everything from the bathhouses in the old country to the difficulties of adjusting to a new country. Once again, Najarian uses the female voice to help him tell his story.

The figure of the mother also dominates Najarian's most recent publication, the 1999 *The Great American Loneliness*. While fear and alienation of life in exile provide the central focus, all is not dark here. The mother brings everything into focus. For example, although the narrator[8] never has a home of his own, he knows that he "could always go home…[to] a strong mother" (Najarian 1999, p. 167). When her son is unable to paint her aiki, she says confidently, 'Give me that brush. I'll do it myself" (Najarian 1999, p. 105). This is the same mother who boldly proclaims in *Daughters of Memory*, "Look at me, I always find something to do. Don't give up, my son, clean your studio if you get lonely, go shopping, cook soup" (Najarian 1986, p. 40). Amidst "the usual fear and the doubt" (Najarian 1999, p. 150) and the panic at the darkness ahead, the mother is a ray of light. To believe in nothing is impossible for her. Her aiki, her "Eden," may have been "lost," but not before it "gave her the roots she could transplant after she was exiled" (Najarian 1999, p. 165). "To those who now lived on her father's aiki," she can say, "Take it, life is more important to me as long as I'm alive I can love it anywhere."

---

[8] *The Great American Loneliness* is the most clearly autobiographical of Najarian's fiction. It is a collection of stories where Najarian puts himself directly and clearly into his writing.

Once, when someone talked to her of suicide, she retorted "How could you kill yourself when your soul is so sweet?" (Najarian 1999, p. 163).

In conclusion, I would like to add that by foregrounding the immigrant woman's voice, a marginalized voice, Najarian validates the existence of "the other." In America, a land where everyone is an orphan, "other" loses its negative connotation of "outsider," of "inferior," and the novel becomes in post-modern critic Homi Bhabha's words, "the great celebrant of the migrant acts of survival" (1994, p. 7). Ultimately, *Voyages* succeeds not because it transmits the Armenian, or the American tradition, but because it recognizes the inextricable, indeed the inevitable, interconnectedness of cultures. That Najarian should make a woman the vehicle for this recognition is highly significant.

Works cited:

Bhabha, Homi. 1994. *The Location of Culture*. New York: Routledge.

Najarian, Peter. 1979. *Voyages*. 2nd ed. New York: Ararat Press.

Najarian, Peter. 1986. *Daughters of Memory: A Story*. Berkeley, CA: City Miner Books.

Najarian, Peter. 1999. *The Great American Loneliness*. Cambridge, MA: Blue Crane Books.

Arpi Sarafian is Lecturer in English Language and Literature at California State University, Los Angeles. She received her doctorate from the University of Southern California. Her work has been published in numerous magazines such as *The Armenian Observer, Ararat*, the *Los Angeles Times, PMLA Journal* (Modern Language Association).

NGO PROGRAMS EMPOWERING WOMEN OF ARMENIA

Armine Ishkanian, moderator

Armenian Women and the NGO Sector: Achievements, Challenges, and Opportunities

Under seventy years of Communist rule, there had been very little space for civil society or for non-governmental/non-Party organizations in Armenia. The intense post-Soviet growth in the number and type of non-governmental organizations (NGOs) in Armenia is both a reaction to the past repression of such activities as well as a response to the new funding that has been made available for NGOs by international agencies and Western governments.

In the post-Soviet period, donors have been motivated to fund NGOs, because NGOs as the civil society organizations par excellence, are perceived as panaceas for the political cynicism, apathy, and over-centralization of the region and as signs of the emerging civil societies in the former Soviet states.

This paper is based on research I conducted in Armenia in 1996, 1997, 1999, and 2000 with two of the most active NGOs, the Armenian Chapter of the Helsinki Citizens' Assembly and the All Armenian Women's Union in the capital Yerevan. I begin by defining what an NGO is and then I go on to discuss the

This article was written while the author was a Visiting Fellow at the Institute of Slavic, East European, and Eurasian Studies at the University of California, Berkeley. She thanks the National Research Council, the International Research and Exchange Board, the Academy of Educational Development, the International Project for Academic Research in the Caucasus, and the University of California, San Diego Department of Anthropology for their generous support that allowed her to conduct research in Armenia.

growth of NGOs in Armenia from 1991 to 2001. I describe their achievements and explore the challenges they will face in coming years.

What is an NGO?

NGOs as a category of organizational entities were created at the founding of the United Nations (UN) over fifty years ago. The category was invented in order to describe a specific relationship between civic organizations and the intergovernmental process. Since then, this term has been applied to organizations that are neither governmental or are part of private industry. Outside of the UN, some of these organizations are referred to as non-profit organizations, as is the case in the US, or simply as civil society organizations. In the former Soviet Union and throughout Latin America, Asia, Africa, and Eastern Europe these organizations are called NGOs and they operate in the sector of civil society or the third sector. The third sector is that which is situated between the first (governmental) and second (private) sectors. Civil society may be considered as a sphere of social interaction between the household and the state, characterized by community co-operation, structures of voluntary association, and networks of public communication. In this sense, civil society is separate from the home, state, political parties, and businesses. Ideally, it is the place or space where concerned citizens can come together to collectively voice their concerns and address and implement projects that enjoy community support—no matter how large or small.

In Armenia, an NGO is an organization that is created by private citizens and is registered with the Ministry of Justice. NGO sizes vary from ten to thousands of members and these groups have different missions and activities that range from providing health care, educational and social services to addressing children's rights, women's rights, helping people find mates, and promoting such diverse initiatives as poverty reduction, civil society and democracy building, and cultural renewal. These organizations are tax-exempt and receive very little, if any, technical or administrative support from the state. The bulk of funding for these organizations comes from foreign or international donors including various UN agencies, the US Agency for International Development, the Eurasia Foundation, the Norwegian Refugee Council, Oxfam, Friedrich Ebert Foundation, etc.

Currently there are over 2,500 NGOs registered with the Armenian Ministry of Justice, and two-thirds of these groups are led by women.

The NGO Sector in Armenia: Why Women?

The fact that the majority of NGO leaders and members in Armenia are women is due to various factors. First, in the early 1990s, the removal of the Soviet quota system led to a sharp decline in the number of women in official positions and although women had been crucial in the independence movement by participating in the demonstrations, work and hunger strikes, making speeches, and collecting money for the effort, once independence was achieved, women found themselves excluded from the new government.[1] NGOs became a popular path for public participation for the women who were excluded from the political parties and government positions.

Second, men were not initially interested in the "non-governmental" sector, since any man who wishes to be active in political or public life can do so through the government or political parties; they do not need NGOs for this purpose. Also many men were not interested in NGOs since the rewards of NGO participation, in terms of grants and micro-credit programs, were too small and the bureaucratic details of operating an NGO were too numerous.

---

[1] In 1985 121 of 219 members of parliament were women. However, it is clear that this was due to an inflated quota system, since once the Soviet system collapsed and a new National Assembly was elected in 1991, the number of female parliamentarians dropped to eight.

Finally, a preference among donors in supporting women's initiatives and organizations has made NGOs a viable alternative for women. The 1995 UN Fourth World Conference on Women in Beijing was a watershed event in the development of women's NGOs in Armenia. Following the conference, the number and type of women's organizations increased dramatically as women who attended the Beijing conference returned to Armenia informed and educated about the global gender discourses, issues, and concerns. The Beijing conference also stimulated greater funding and interest in regards to the role of women in development and the transitions on the part of donors who proclaimed women as the more "cost-effective" beneficiaries of development and civil society aid. (Buvini'c 1996)

As women have become the leaders in Armenia's NGO sector in the last ten years, they have played a key role in Armenia's post-Soviet transition as intermediaries between the global and local levels. In this capacity, women NGO leaders have been instrumental in translating, adopting, and reconciling foreign models and approaches to the local context. Women's NGOs and women-led NGOs have sponsored various initiatives, including promoting the establishment of civil society and democratic institutions and practices, sponsoring poverty reduction and sustainable economic development programs, developing health care, educational, and social service initiatives, and working to better the lives of children, women, refugees, the elderly, and other socio-economically vulnerable groups.

There are many examples of successful women-led NGO projects. For instance, in the field of civil society and democracy development, the Helsinki Citizens' Assembly NGO led by Anahit Bayandur and Natalya Martirossian has worked to assist refugees, promote peace and conflict resolution in Karabagh, and to promote civic initiatives in the four provincial cities of

Charentsavan, Ijevan, Kapan, and Vanadzor. The HCA's civic
initiative programs advocate an approach in which citizens are
encouraged and supported in playing an active role in the development of their communities.

In the field of health care, the Yerevan based Women's Health
Care Association, led by Hranoush Hakobian, has worked with
its US-based partner, the Armenian American Cultural Association, Inc., a 501 (c) (3) non-profit organization led by Rita Balian,
to establish the Armenian American Mammography University
Center (AAMUC) in Yerevan. Since 1997, the AAMUC has provided over 30,000 women with free or low-cost mammography
and ultrasound breast cancer screenings that have saved the lives
of hundreds of women.

The Armenian International Women's Association, a
transnational organization that has chapters in the US and Armenia, has also been very active in promoting health initiatives
as it has helped sponsor the Yerevan Center for Women's Reproductive Health which is aimed at improving the level of
health care available for women in Armenia.

In the field of education and children's issues, the All Armenian Women's Union, led by former First Lady Ludmilla Ter-
Petrossian, helped establish the Oshagan Children's Rehabilitation Center for physically and mentally disabled children and
has worked with other sponsors to support the work of the
Kharbert and Vanadzor Orphanages. In 1996, because of
AAWU's efforts, the Armenian National Assembly adopted the
law protecting the rights of children.

In the area of women's issues, NGOs such as the Center for
Gender Studies of the Democracy Union (led by Gulnara
Shahinian), the Association of Women with University Education (led by Jemma Hasratian), the Women's Republican Council (led by Nora Hakobian), the Women's Rights Center (led by
Susanna Vardanyan), and the Maternity Fund of Armenia (led
by Susanna Aslanyan), among others have been instrumental

in drawing attention to various socio-economic problems facing women including poverty, unemployment, discrimination, domestic violence, etc. These NGOs have conducted research, organized conferences and roundtable seminars, and published reports, articles, and books to inform the public, policy makers, and government officials about these problems and to begin the work of finding sustainable solutions.

There are many other successful NGO projects, which I have described elsewhere. (Ishkanian, 2000)

Conclusion

Over the last decade Armenia's NGOs have built up great human, leadership, and knowledge resources. As we move into the 21st century, however, it is increasingly clear, especially after September 11, how problems once thought to be bounded in particular local contexts are now transnational in nature and scope. Armenia's NGOs have new challenges ahead of them in defining, studying, and addressing problems and issues that are not contained in national borders but yet fundamentally impact the lives of their constituents.

Given the existing level of communication and collaboration between Armenian women in Armenia and their counterparts in the Armenian diaspora communities in the United States, Europe, and the Middle East, there is a basis for transnational cooperative efforts. How these groups, through further concerted collaborative efforts, will address the transnational problems of the sexual trafficking of women and girls, the illegal labor migration and its impact on women and children, the illegal adoption of Armenian children, and other transnational problems remains to be seen.

Works cited:

Buvini'c, Mayra, Catherine Gwin, and Lisa M. Bates. 1996. *Investing in Women: Progress and Prospects for the World Bank.* Washington, D.C.: Published by the Overseas Development Council in cooperation with the International Center for

Research on Women; Baltimore, MD: Distributed by the Johns Hopkins University Press

Ishkanian, Armine. 2000. "Hearths and Modernity: the Role of Women in NGOs in Post-Soviet Armenia." Ph.D. dissertation, University of California, San Diego

Armine Ishkanian is a Postdoctoral Research Fellow at the UC Berkeley Institute of Slavic, East European, and Eurasian Studies. Her dissertation, "Hearths and Modernity: the Role of Women in NGOs in Post-Soviet Armenia," examines the role of women in NGOs in Armenia. In Spring 2002 she taught a course titled, "Women in the Caucasus and Central Asia" in the UCB Department of International and Area Studies. She has published many articles on the role of women in Armenia and is currently working on a book that examines the role of women in Armenia's post-Soviet transition 1991-2001.

Domestic and Social Issues

Jemma Ananyan, moderator

My Wishes for the Armenian Woman in the Twenty-first Century

The Armenian nation has started and finished the twentieth century with genocide: the beginning of the century opened with the infamous genocide of the Turkish Armenians, and the end of the century closed with the tragic deaths of Armenians in Azerbaijan in Sumgait. Thus, in the history of the world nations, Armenian women rank high among those who have lost sons, husbands, and fathers and have cried over these losses. My wish is that no mines will burst in the souls of Armenian women, since the explosion of mines in the soul will leave terrible ruins. Grigor Zohrap said that a woman is a laugh herself; she should not be changed into tears. I wish that this were true.

My wish is that an independent Armenia in the twenty-first century will have a strong economy. Only this will stop the migration of men out of Armenia, and no longer will there be women waiting for their sons and husbands to return.

There is a saying that one good man is just a good man, but one good woman is her whole family. I wish that our sisters in the diaspora, as worthy Armenian women, will create strong Armenian families that speak the Armenian language, keep Armenian customs and traditions, and day by day make stronger their ties with their motherland.

Today, unfortunately, the criterion for all values is money. I wish for all Armenian women that their Armenian motherland, and not money, would be the criterion for all of their values.

I wish that in the twenty-first century, the Armenian woman can live a life without suffering, which allows her to express her talent and to understand dignity.

Jemma Ananyan is the former mayor of the town of Ijevan and has been a member of the Armenian National Assembly. She is currently an advisor to the Minister of Social Welfare.

Reflections on the Subjugation of Armenian Women

Eva Medzorian

My close relationship with Armenia began in 1972, when I took my first of more than fifty trips to Armenia. Most troubling for me was to see a visible double standard in Armenia, where men enjoyed a special camaraderie with one another that did not include women. Women were expected to rear the children, run the household, be submissive, feminine, and leave the important decision-making to the men.

In the mid 1980s, I was invited to an informal meeting to meet representatives of various women's organizations. Soon, a well-dressed, middle-aged male member of Parliament appeared. He read an extremely lengthy, boring speech about women's issues. The women sat docile and politely listened. I whispered into the ear of my hostess, "Why is this man speaking for the women? Can't the women speak for themselves?" She answered, "This is the way it is here—protocol." When he finished and left, the atmosphere warmed, and we were finally able to get acquainted with one another. We shared mutual concerns and enjoyed intelligent conversation, which bridged our eastern and western mentalities. We had found each other and regarded each other as family. I did not want that afternoon to end and thought, "If only there were a women's organization to provide a forum for interaction and networking for Armenian women worldwide." I searched for such an organization but found none. In 1990, I discussed my idea with two local acquaintances in Boston, Barbara Merguerian and Olga Proudian, and together we founded the Armenian International Women's Association. Our diverse backgrounds were a perfect blend for the kind of non-political, non-sectarian organization we envisioned that would be able to bring together all Armenian women.

Even in the 1990s, Armenian women found themselves lost in the endless shuffle of male-dominated politics. Painfully, most women could go only so far until they were stopped by an invisible barrier. It was important for me to learn more about our past, in order to understand how we came to the present impasse and how to prepare ourselves for a brighter future.

Some early examples of the subjugation of Armenian women can be traced back to the twelfth century when Vardapets Poghos Taroneci (1123) and Mkhitar Gosh (1213) rejected the renewal of the office of deaconess in the Armenian Church, which had fallen into decline. Women during that period were called upon to serve the church as deaconesses only when the priests or deacons were in dire need of help. Man was considered perfect, while woman was considered imperfect. In the Mkhitar Gosh Manual of Rules (*Datastanagirk*), women were forbidden to give evidence in courtrooms and were not even permitted to crush the grapes used to prepare communion wine. Women could not become godmothers at baptism rites, because the church did not allow them to serve as guarantors or witnesses. The *vardapets* justified their argument by preaching that it was not proper for a woman to remain in church during baptism, because the Virgin Mother of the Lord was not present at Christ's baptism in the Jordan River.

Even in the wedding ceremony, the priest reminds the groom that he is the active head of the family and that the bride is directed to be a passive partner. Two years ago in Watertown,

Massachusetts, I heard a young, unmarried deacon preach that it was important for a woman to be subordinate in all things relating to her husband and her church.

It is especially disturbing that even today there are older Armenian women who advocate that women should be seen and not heard. An ethnographist in Armenia noted, "Women in the past were praised in song and poetry for their physical beauty, love and passion, but not for their intelligence. She was thought of as a man's possession, to be protected and loved." Women were expected to be absorbed totally by motherhood, their household responsibilities, and their commitment to preserve and transfer Armenian traditions from the past to the present.

Serpouhi Dussap, born in Constantinople in 1840, wrote on the myth of equality between men and women. "What kind of equality is that which places half of humanity at the feet of males? What kind of liberty is that which deprives women of the ability to protest, to act and to initiate?" she asked. What is the power, she added, that tells men, "Act fearlessly, you are free," and to women, "Cherish your chains uncomplainingly?"

In 1859, John Stuart Mill published his essay, "On Liberty." He wrote that the "legal subordination of one sex to the other is wrong in itself, and now one of the chief hindrances to human improvement; and it ought to be replaced by a principle of perfect equality, admitting no power or privilege on the one side, nor disability on the other."

In 1918, Armenia was one of the first countries in the world to adopt legislation ensuring the women's right to vote and participate in government. Women did not receive the right to vote in the United States until two years later, in 1920.

Freedom of speech, open elections, judicial, land and business reforms began to be introduced into the Republic of Armenia nearly a decade ago, when this fledgling democracy declared its independence from the Soviet Republic on September 21,

1991. Yet, women were not encouraged to reach coveted high places in government and in business. Sadly, today's Armenia does not have one Armenian woman appointed in the government ministry. Traditional men and women still believe that it is not feminine for a woman to go into political or business life. I have heard men say, "Women should not take jobs away from men." This attitude caused the intellectuals to suffer, the middle class to sink into poverty, and it allowed for the poor to get poorer and the rich to get richer.

A closed society for seventy years, Armenia was suddenly exposed for the last ten years to western style television and Hollywood movies featuring sex and violence, bizarre musicians, sadistic ways, and pornography. Casinos opened up everywhere in the heart of Yerevan. Six months ago, I heard a paid advertisement on Armenian radio: "If you want to enjoy all of the pleasures of a woman's body for just $3.00, come to our club." Women protested, and the advertisement was removed. Even in the United States, men made crude jokes at cocktail parties about how to handle a woman. "Keep her barefoot and pregnant," they would joke. They stopped only after women objected.

Though a traditional Armenian husband may be well educated and industrious, he also may be patronizing, condescending and demonstrate dictatorial attitudes toward his wife. The modern Armenian man should accept a woman as his equal. Unfortunately, modern western culture has discarded most of the rituals of the past, leaving its citizens adrift and vulnerable to dangerous new life styles. Some wealthy parents have overindulged their children with excessive luxuries, creating an uncontrollable, spoiled youth.

Four months ago, I was walking up Abovian Street just past the elegantly redone Yerevan Hotel. I saw two teenage boys jumping from one sculpted figurine to the other figurine in the dry fountain that was being refurbished. A woman wearily sat on the edge of the fountain, with her head in her hands, oblivious to what was going on around her. I asked the boys to step out of the fountain so that we could talk. They wanted to know what I was looking at. I told them I was admiring the old fountain, because I had never seen a fountain so beautiful. I remarked, "You are so lucky to have something that beautiful in Yerevan, because back in my home town we do not have a fountain as unique as yours." I asked if they noticed the broken piece on the fountain. They said that they did not break it. I asked them to protect the fountain from harm because this was their city. They asked me to look across the street and tell them if the ultra modern, glass disco café, recently remodeled, is also beautiful. I said, "No, it's ugly because it does not fit in with the beautiful old Yerevan architecture." They clapped their hands and did a little dance. They came over and vigorously shook my hand and said, "Don't worry, auntie, we will take care of this fountain." They gave me a big ear-to-ear smile and walked away. They needed their self worth to be valued and elevated. The street children of Armenia are a totally new phenomenon brought about by the economic crisis.

Many women are poor, horribly overburdened, and have difficulty finding enough food for their children, let alone the ability to clothe and educate them. Abortions are appallingly high in number because, in large part, men do not want to take away from their pleasure by using contraceptives.

Prostitution appealed to some women as the only way to solve their desperate situation. Some young girls, trapped by heartless men and women who promised them the moon, were taken to such countries as Turkey, Iran, and Dubai, where their passports were confiscated. Raped, ravaged, and left penniless, they were forced to work as prostitutes.

Armenian wives have also had to deal with their husbands taking mistresses. Long a hidden subject, and much too shameful to talk about, many wives turn a blind eye, as long as their husbands take financial care of their children and household.

These men may contract sexually transmitted diseases from many partners, pass these diseases to their wives, and then blame the wives.

Some wealthy men pick out young women to escort around town to show how powerful they are, with no sense of shame. "Attractive young women under the age of twenty-five, with good figures and wearing short skirts, have taken over the job market," lamented an attractive, thirty-five-year-old mother who said employers considered her too old to work for them.

Professor Joyce Fletcher, of Boston's Simmons Graduate School of Management and a research scholar at Wellesley College, was recently interviewed in *The Boston Globe* about her new book, *Disappearing Acts*. She stated, "Our image of leaders and managers is still very masculine—we confuse masculinity with good work." She said that important training needed for the workplace is concentrated among women who are successful homemakers, community volunteers, and care givers. Fletcher said, "The problem is that we don't think of them right now as organizational skills. Traditionally, we have thought that growth is a process of separating ourselves from others and becoming more independent, but when you listen to women's experience, you see that growth is interactive and relational." Relational skills, important for a business to grow more successfully, can bring about a clearer understanding of masculinity and femininity.

We need to set good examples starting from the heads of families, to the heads of clergy, and to the heads of governments. Courageous, selfless acts of compassion, kindness, and wisdom, along with intelligence and experience, are needed to build a civil society, where women must be included in all of the important decision making.

Eva Medzorian is AIWA's co-founder and first president, past vice-president of the Cambridge-Yerevan Sister City Association, and chairs the Armenian School Aid Project. She is a recognized community leader and Co-Chair of AIWA's Third International Conference.

Violence Against Women in Armenia

Susanna Vardanyan

Socio-economic Implications

It seems strange to ordinary citizens, as well as to officials, that when we discuss the issue of violence against women in Armenia many people do not acknowledge the fact of violence.

Such an approach is explained mainly by the mentality of the society rather than by the situation that there is really no violence against women in our society. Consequently, the perception of violence against women is a relatively new phenomenon, an issue which the society is unwilling to admit to and be conscious of. The traditionally accepted role of a woman in the family interferes with the full awareness by society of the existing major problem of violence.

Armenia is a country in which the family is considered a private sphere and domestic violence is treated as the family's internal affair and not as a violation of human rights. Some men consider women as a certain type of property when they can. These men will exercise power over them in all matters (within the family and outside it) and are typical of that kind of mentality. An approach like this is common for families where women are dependent on their husbands both materially and financially. Women try to come to terms with that and usually put up with violations, as there is no way out.

Today there is no legal protection and there are no adequate laws to guarantee concrete punitive measures against domestic violence. There is no alternative governmental or non-governmental protection that can provide women suffering from domestic violence with alternative asylum and there are no possibilities to provide employment.

Socio-economic crises cause families to fall apart. Cases when a woman becomes the head of the family and shoulders the responsibility for her children all alone are not rare. The phenomenon of male unemployment shocks the psychology of a woman and results in domestic conflicts and violations. The new conditions result in new interrelations in the family.

Survey Description and Outcome

Seeking to determine whether in our society violence against women is a rule rather than an exception, the NGO Women's Rights Center conducted a sociological survey to obtain accurate answers to the following questions:

- Is violence an issue in Armenia?
- What are the prevailing forms of violence in Armenia?
- What kinds of violence is a woman subject to in the family, at work and in social circles?
- How does violence affect the psychology and social state of a woman?
- What everyday problems serve as causes for oppression and violations?
- Is such treatment a result of tradition or the current situation?
- How do women expect to improve the current situation?

The survey was conducted during July and August 2000 in Yerevan, in middle-size towns—Gyumri, Vanadzor, Yeghegnadzor, Noyemberyan, Goris, Aparan, Armavir, Gavar—and in neighboring villages—Hatsik, Vahagni, Vernashen, Berdavan, Kornidzor, Moulki, Hoktember, Noradouz. A total of 1,200 women, selected according to gender distinctions, age group, educational level and location, were surveyed.

The survey found that 74 percent were subject to violence, out of which:

1. Psychological violence (abuse, brutality) 40 percent
2. Physical violence (blows, beating, torture) 19 percent
3. Sexual violence 15 percent

Family members and relatives committed the overwhelming majority of violations.

The women surveyed were asked to assess their family climate in recent years: What was it like and how had it changed?

It turned out that the number of families experiencing tension in relations had increased by 22 percent, while the number of families with good relationships had decreased by the same percentage. The portion of families where there were aggravated relations had reached 57 percent.

Summing up the data from questions of this group we conclude that general socio-economic conditions have significantly increased tensions in the family situation and in some cases have caused families to separate.

According to poll results, the socio-economic situation of the last ten years on the whole has affected Armenian women in the following way—only 4 percent of women have benefited from the opportunities provided by economic and political systems, while the social expectations of 95 percent of women were not met.

Our aim was to find out the reasons for disputes and conflicts. There are three main reasons:

1. Harsh socio-economic conditions 49 percent
2. The low level of tradition and family life 25 percent
3. The relationships between spouses 18 percent

Unfortunately, domestic disputes take place mostly in the presence of children; in every fourth case the children become the witnesses of the most unpleasant incidents in family life; particularly, cases of the woman's humiliation. So it is obvious that the incorporation of violence as an inseparable part of life takes root in childhood.

According to frequency of violations, women are divided into the following groups:

Subject to violence	Percentage of women
1-3 times / lifetime	53.5
1-3 times / year	23.0
1-3 times / month	14.0
1-3 times / week	9.5

Most cases of humiliation are committed by family members and close relatives (19 percent), four times more than by others (4.5 percent). At the same time, 90 percent of cases of everyday humiliation (including the major part of rapes) take place in families and only 10 percent in public places. All this underlines the fact that women become targets for violence in the family.

The most important part of the investigation deals with how humiliation affects the psychology of women. According to the findings of the survey, humiliation had a negative after-effect upon 57.7 percent of women, moreover, 3.1 percent of women had tried to commit suicide. Present below are some stories noted by the respondents in the questionnaire:

- "Knife wounds all over my body, my face covered with bruises. Because of heavy blows, part of my head seemed to have turned to mush, and all these are the consequences of the so-called love of my husband. I have a constant feeling of fear. My life is meaningless. I tried to commit suicide several times, but did not have enough courage to do so."

- "Maybe the biggest mistake was that I married a man I didn't love. Our married life together started out with humiliation. My husband used to think that I had no right to speak out or express an opinion. I became his servant, his slave. If I happened to forget my "place," he used to remind me of it by beating and cursing. All these continue until today. I have a feeling that my life was in vain. I live only for my children's sake."

- K., 28 years old. " There was a time I was head over heels in love with him, but when I became his wife, he started persecuting, humiliating me. I'm tired. From time to time I think of committing suicide or leaving him. I'll become a criminal one day, take revenge or harm myself."

It is obvious that violence causes a stressful situation and in several cases an inclination to suicide. It should be noted, that some groups of women (rural women, women with secondary education) avoided answering these types of questions. This indicates conscious and subconscious syndromes in them.

We were interested to learn what expectations Armenian women had for the future. The results are as follows:

1. Pessimists   47 percent
2. Optimists   42 percent
3. No orientation   11 percent

In fact, feelings are more inclined to somber moods, but this inclination is not yet so great as to be perceived as a national calamity.

Conclusions

Domestic violence as a phenomenon exists in Armenia, and the general conditions in our country contribute to its growth. Violence is demonstrated in all forms—psychological, physical and sexual. It covers all sections of the population irrespective of age, educational level, economic conditions and employment.

Unfortunately, ways of forestalling violence and the existing mechanisms of punishing the crime remain ineffective. Non-governmental organizations must teach what women's rights are, which will finally result in the equitable settlement of problems of existing violations against women.

Suggestions

Summing up the situation existing in the sphere of violence against women in Armenia and taking into account our right to be free from violence, we draw the conclusion that women are in a triangle, where there are:

- Family laws in the first corner
- Society laws in the second corner
- State laws in the third corner

To prevent and reduce violence, it is necessary to improve the above-mentioned structure. The state, including the courts, must protect women's rights against any type of violence. We must take part in the process of forestalling violence in our country and in drafting and improving laws punishing violence. The next important factor is to create opportunities for women to work and to give them the ability to be economically independent.

Violence against women is offensive to our dignity and creates obstacles for a woman to become a full and equal member of society. Our purpose is to help them. It would be easier to achieve this goal, if we made our cooperation even stronger, and hopefully this significant conference will contribute to it as well.

Susanna Vardanyan is the president of the Women's Rights Center, a Yerevan-based Non-Governmental Organization.

The Present Difficulties of the Armenian Woman

Elizaveta Danielyan

The Armenian woman is in a very difficult situation today and has numerous problems. On the one hand, she has to keep the gift of maternity given her by nature. It is her role to give birth to the next generation; to do her best to maintain a kind and close family atmosphere; and to raise her children. On the other hand, she must earn a living like a man and support her family financially, because at present most of the husbands of these women are jobless.

It is cruel for young Armenian women to endure the absence of their husbands when these men leave to earn a living in remote countries. Armenian women are responsible for caring for their children as well as their elderly relatives. With their husbands away for extended periods of time, women alone shoulder the problems of their families. Without two parents, a family loses its real face and sense. Ideally, children need to be brought up by both their mother and father, in order to be healthy, wealthy, kind, and useful members of society.

The Armenian woman is ready to stand all kinds of tests and to overcome many difficulties in order to keep the traditional Armenian family strong, healthy and prosperous. She does not work for her pleasure, nor is she able to pursue her favorite activities. Instead, she takes jobs which may not suit her for the sake of her family's survival.

It is very painful, and to my mind, there is nothing more awful nor difficult, when our nice, pretty, educated, honest and modest girls and women have to leave Armenia to gain employment—often, for example, as nurses or housekeepers—abroad.

The Armenian woman has a great, creative spirit, but she has no opportunity to reveal it. The doors of the scientific research institutes have been closed to her. The main features of the Armenian woman's nature—tenderness, common sense, sentimentality, sensitivity, patience, obedience, and hope—are still in effect, but they are bruised due to the troubled social and economic situation in Armenia.

Despite these challenging problems and more, the Armenian woman is never depressed, disappointed, nor is she in despair. She always tries to seek a way out of these difficulties. As she is tested, the Armenian woman stands proudly. She knows that the most important and urgent task is to ensure the availability of work. The Armenian woman today knows that only by hard work will it be possible to create a healthy family and a secure lifestyle.

Elizaveta Danielyan chairs the First Instance Court, Ajapneak and Davitashen communities, in Yerevan, Armenia.

Women and Politics

Alvina Gyulumian, moderator

Rising to the Challenge: Women in the Political Process

Linda J. Melconian

Representative democracy is an effective system for guaranteeing and protecting rights to people who are allowed to participate in it. First, through the legislature, and then through enforcement by the courts and other executive officers, individuals gain the right to equal protection under the law. Equal rights then lead (very slowly in some cases) to real rights—to treatment as first class citizens with a full voice and stake in society.

In the United States, women's involvement in the political process has proceeded in fits and starts. We first gained the right to vote in 1920 but have been very slow to take the next step—from spectators who merely vote, to participants who have an active role as elected officials. After all, in the words of Jeanette Rankin, the first women elected to Congress in 1917: "We're half the people; we should be half the Congress." Today, the United States has 9 female members out of 100 in the US Senate and 56 female members out of 435 in the House of Representatives. America has never elected or appointed a female President, Speaker or Chief Justice of the Supreme Court.

The news at the state level has been only marginally better. While Arizona recently elected a full slate of female constitutional officers, in my own home state of Massachusetts—long considered one of the more progressive in the nation—women represent just a quarter of the elected legislature. We have recently elected a female Treasurer and Lieutenant Governor, but we have never elected a female Governor, Senate President or Speaker of the House. Last year, for the first time our Governor nominated a woman to lead one of the three branches of government. Margaret Marshall, as Chief Justice of the Massachusetts Supreme Judicial Court, now heads the judiciary. However, Massachusetts has advanced a number of issues of vital importance to women, including inserting an Equal Rights Amendment to our state constitution and passing numerous anti-discrimination measures.

So why is it that women have not been more active participants in the political process? In the United States we have effectively exercised our right to organize around issues that matter to us but have been much slower in gaining a seat at the table where the decisions are made.

What are the barriers for women to full participation in the process? Naturally, there are no simple answers to this question but four factors spring to mind; ignorance and prejudice, absence of role models, lack of initiative, and insufficient information.

Prejudice is still a rampant force in American society and throughout the world. Too often, women are seen as weak, ineffectual, or unable to put together a coalition or handle the challenges of leadership. Too often, governing is seen as a game women don't know how to play.

The absence of female role models in the political process contributes to the problem. We all need trailblazers at the highest levels to break down those barriers of prejudice. It is important to prove that women can and should be involved in the process that shapes their lives and simply to make other women think, "Hey! I can do that too."

In too many cases we have not taken this initiative. We must nurture in ourselves and in our daughters a desire to reach for the stars and not to let anything or anyone hold us back because when we reach for the stars sometimes we catch a falling star. We must become risk takers. As a child growing up, I remember my parents telling me I should think of myself as "Linda Jean Melconian Unlimited." I said it enough times that I began to believe it. We all need to practice that statement. "I am Unlimited." We must continue to take risks because we cannot achieve what we do not attempt. Any one who has not failed has never really tried.

The final barrier we face is lack of information. It is my contention that information is the key to our involvement in the process. Educating women—not just to become legislators but to become effective, persuasive legislators—is the key to overcoming all these barriers. Information sharing creates a beneficial cycle. Through information women are able to gain elected office. Once in office, through hard work and competence we are able to overcome prejudice and ignorance and become role models. Finally, we are able to share this information with other women, bringing more of us into the process, overcoming our reluctance to run, and starting the cycle again.

So as part of this effort to educate and bring more women into public service, let me share some of the lessons I learned in my four-year effort to pass a comprehensive measure to protect the citizens of Massachusetts from discrimination based on their genetic code and prevent public disclosure of the information gained from genetic tests. Each of these parts was critical but it was especially important to establish a right of privacy for this genetic information and make it accessible only with the citizen's consent.

Lesson 1: The Issue

The first step is to pick an important and necessary issue in which you have strong feelings and passions. In many ways you will live and breathe this issue. You will have to understand it inside and out and be willing to talk about it constantly and with whomever will listen.

More importantly, the issue must be one of great personal importance to you. You will literally imprint your blood, sweat and tears on this law. If you don't ultimately care about it, you will achieve only a hollow victory.

Genetic privacy became a passion for me because I view it as the 21st century form of discrimination. I do not have to tell anyone in this room about discrimination or annihilation because of who or what you are. We worked for generations to ban discrimination in all its pernicious forms—I refuse to allow it back under the pretense of scientific advancement. I also know that genetic information is some of the most personal and private information we have. It tells us about diseases to which we are vulnerable and may someday tell us everything from our possible intelligence to our potential lifespan. It should be private.

Lesson 2: Coalition Building

Your efforts may be the catalyst for filing legislation and getting the ball rolling but no piece of legislation is ever passed though the efforts of a single individual. You must build a coalition of advocates, of academics and of fellow legislators. These are people with whom you have shared concerns and interest and who will work with you to pass legislation.

In the case of genetic testing I owe a debt of gratitude to a number of different groups, chiefly our advocates in the Jewish community. Their background and familiarity with historic examples of genetic discrimination made them natural messengers regarding genetic discrimination. Their efforts helped to inform legislators about a difficult and complex issue.

Lesson 3: Understanding the Big Picture

Simply building a group of people who support passage of legislation is often not enough. It is vital to be aware of potential pitfalls and take advantage of outside events that support your cause.

It took two legislative terms to pass genetic testing. The first term we were able to successfully pass the bill in the Senate (our higher legislative branch) but because our House of Representatives (our lower branch) is more conservative, the bill died. The second legislative session I took extra time with the bill in the Senate, working with advocates who supported the bill and members of the insurance industry who opposed the bill, to craft a piece of legislation that would pass not only in the Senate but also in the House.

Our coalition was also able to take advantage of fortunate circumstances. As the genetic testing legislation was awaiting action in the House scientists announced a huge advance in genetic technology, the mapping of the human gene code. This announcement highlighted the potential dangers (as well as the benefits) of genetics. Its timing helped to create a sense of urgency to provide the protections guaranteed under our bill. We were able to use this increased awareness to our advantage to pass the bill in the House.

Lesson 4: Perseverance

My fourth and final lesson is that gaining passage of any piece of legislation is a long and arduous process. You must commit to the effort and not get discouraged. A bill rarely becomes reality the first time you file it. It takes years to increase people's understanding of a problem and to convince them that you have the best solution. It also takes considerable time to create a large coalition with a similar understanding of the issue.

As I mentioned before it took four years and countless hours of work convincing, negotiating and explaining to bring the right of privacy of genetic testing to fruition. I can tell you it is very rewarding to playing the leading role in the passage of important legislation is highly rewarding.

My advice to you is simple. Find an important problem to solve, build a coalition around solving it, keep an eye out both for pitfalls and for opportunities and most importantly, persevere to achieve your goal.

I hope my example today will prove useful to you as you pursue your own legislative goals and political activities. Obstacles confront you at every stage. But remember we are all equal and you are equal to the fight. I want to leave you with a few words from Winston Churchill as you begin the difficult task ahead of you. "Never give in, never give in, never, never, never, never—in nothing great or small, large or petty—never give in except to convictions of honor and good sense."

Linda Melconian is the Majority Leader of the Senate of the Commonwealth of Massachusetts, the first woman to hold that position. She earned her *Juris Doctor* from George Mason University. Her leadership established the Children's Trust Fund to combat child abuse and enabled individuals with HIV/AIDS to receive insurance coverage for medications. She has worked to increase access to health and medical care for women, children, and the elderly. Her annual golf tournament raises money for Battered Women's Shelters.

The Prerequisites for the Realization of National Interests on the Eve of the Twenty-first Century

Naira Melkoumian

The twenty-first century brings about new challenges and to overcome them the unification of the nation is not enough. One should have a clear understanding of national interests and create the necessary prerequisites for implementing them. The formation of a civil society and its consolidation with moral and psychological norms is one of the most important among those. It is necessary to realize that the implementation of national interests, especially in the sphere of foreign policy, is not solely conditioned by political, military and economic factors, but also by its firmness, its ability to withstand the internal and external quakes.

Today, perhaps the time has not come yet to celebrate victories and sum up results. Some people think that all the problems are solved, and that Nagorno Karabagh (Artsakh), the pivotal national interest issue, is free and invulnerable. Today, the security of Nagorno Karabagh is not threatened by an outside enemy. As surprising as this may sound, it is threatened by our people's loss of duty towards its past, misgivings about our own capabilities, and eventually pessimism, that corrodes the basis of our national home.

We have no right to forget that we are still on our way towards an aim. We have no right to destroy the spiritual potential of our nation, which allowed Armenia, one of the few ancient states of the same age with European civilization, to carry
on its existence also into the third millenium. There was a time,
perhaps, when we could take pride in this fact. Most importantly, we could use that experience to resist the historical or-
deals that we were subjected to for centuries. But now it has
become unfashionable to even remember that. But I think that
right now, on the eve of the festive celebrations devoted to the
1700th anniversary of adopting Christianity as a state religion
in Armenia and establishing its statehood, we need the world
to see this very quality of ours. And, in general, I think the coming years should become "years of discovering Armenia"—the
"discovery" of our spiritual world, culture, and the unique secret of our national longevity.

In the given circumstances a question arises: do we know
ourselves, do we respect our viability? If we listen to today's
Armenians, then the answer we hear is no. And that's where it
hurts me most. In the current atmosphere of foreign affairs, our
faith in ourselves, our self-respect, and our national pride became the factors determining the preservation of Artsakh—our
main national interest.

Since 1988 the hopes and thoughts of the Armenian people
were concentrated on Nagorno Karabagh. All able forces of the
nation were brought together to implement the most important
task of gaining freedom and independence for Artsakh and ensuring its security. On our way to it we had to overcome the
stages of war, post-war rehabilitation, peace-building and internal crisis, consistently solving a range of military, political,
diplomatic and economic problems. As a result, it is the tenth
year already that Nagorno Karabagh lives with an independent
life from Azerbaijan. While recognizing the courage and hero-
ism of Karabaghis who defended their tiny homeland by shed-

ding their blood, I would like to point out that without Armenia's and the diaspora's full support and unity of all parts of the Armenian people, the gaining of real independence for Artsakh would have proved more difficult.

Let us also not forget that a serious political attitude was formed towards Karabagh only after the sudden change on the front, when the so-called Nagorno Karabagh Autonomous Region was liberated and the land-link reestablished with Armenia. That is why all diplomatic efforts to solve the problem should be directed at the created reality of Nagorno Karabagh being a serious geopolitical factor, until the status of Nagorno Karabagh is internationally recognized. This is the principal position of the authorities of the Nagorno Karabagh Republic.

In essence, ethno-territorial demarcation took place in the region between the Armenians and the Azeris. A breach of this is full of danger for the future and threatens constant instability. No one speaks loudly of this fact today. But it is a reality that should be taken into consideration. Because our region, unlike other places, has very recently entered a period that has just ended in Europe, for example.

If the international community tries to make the Caucasus a stable, peaceful and predictable region, it should seek decisions that would confirm the demarcations that have already taken place, simultaneously not hindering the balance of geopolitical interests in the region.

I have to note with great regret that during the first stage of the renewal of the Karabagh conflict and in the years of the enforced war, the Armenian people defended their national interests predominantly thanks to their great internal potential. However, that potential, having not fully exhausted itself, does not seem to be showing its worth today—in peacetime. Re-thinking and reviving that internal potential is the imperative of the day. Those tendencies are obvious in the recently much spoken problem of immigration.

I can declare with full confidence that a certain social tension, insufficient employment and, as a result, changes in the demographic situation in the Republic are characteristic and even normal for post-Soviet countries in transition. In addition to those problems, I would even say that disease is a distinctive feature for all states that had recently gained independence. Even powerful Russia, with its economic and scientific potential, and comparably well off countries of Eastern Europe could not avoid those problems. Not to mention that the international organizations are currently working out certain programs to stop the "brain drain" from those countries and that there are suggestions of initiating similar programs for Armenia.

I am convinced that not only the authorities, but the whole system of our society including the political parties and politicians, should take the burden of undertaking an objective analysis of the reasons and consequences of that phenomenon. Unfortunately, we have chosen a different way. Instead of impartially analyzing and deciding the objective and subjective reasons for what has happened and taking necessary measures to improve the situation, some extremely patriotic people are guided by a mere political conjunctivitis. The impression is formed that in their actions and statements that they are guided by the yellow press principle, "The best news is bad news." In their speeches from different platforms they confirm that the country is in an irreversible decline and there is not even a flash of hope for its revival. Absurd statements are made that Armenia is not a good place in which to live. And they argue that the government is implementing a deliberate genocide of its own nation. We deplore the careless use of the notion of genocide, which recalls painful memories in our national consciousness, by misguided people with half-open eyes. And a question arises: don't those people understand that with such statements they worsen the situation even more, don't they imagine what may be the results of such an immense negative influence and that by deliberately injecting those ideas into our peoples minds they humiliate our diaspora?

I am also ready to declare without question, that in a free civil society, freedom of speech is of absolute importance, and maybe, the most visible and tangible success in the years of independence. We cannot ignore the fact that the authorities, both in Armenia and Karabagh, fully realize the importance of the choice of democracy as a means of defending their national interests. On that road there may be mistakes and omissions but the most important thing is to aspire not to withdraw from the chosen course.

Without a doubt, the current level of the developed society allows us to ensure a detailed control over every single step and any undertaking of the authorities. More so, both in Armenia and Karabagh, deputies have been elected who can fully control the actions of the executive leadership. We cannot allow the freedom of self-expression to turn into a struggle against our statehood. Both inside and outside the country, serious as well as absolutely artificial problems are brought to the public consciousness for consideration.

To support my observations, I will bring only one of the numerous examples. International observers present at the Karabagh parliamentary elections in June 2001, made an interesting remark in the conclusion of their report, that after the elections, described by authoritative observers as free and fair, some people at the central electoral committee who had arrived from Yerevan "pressed the international observers for criticism of the Karabagh poll."

I would like to repeat that the realization of our national interests, especially in the sphere of foreign policy, is not solely conditioned by political, military and economic factors, but also by its firmness, its ability to withstand the internal and external quakes.

Despite the hardships we face today, we are gradually getting closer to the aim for which heroes sacrificed their lives, soldiers fought battles, and women and children suffered, i.e. all those who did not leave the country during those difficult years. Those who were with us in spirit and heart, who sincerely supported us, who lightened our hardships and the heavy weight of our losses, helped us to resist and win a victory. Having paid a very high price for the freedom of Artsakh we have no right to waste the fruits of our not easily gained victory.

I have addressed a topic that is usually not spoken about and is, so to speak, an issue of our internal kitchen, at the Armenian International Women's Association's Conference. I have no doubt that Armenian women who did not hesitate to arm and who underwent so many hardships are, today, also capable of overcoming the unclear marathon of self-destruction whereby everyone tries to be a step ahead of others. I am more than convinced that today our homeland needs the sincere efforts of Armenian women directed at the preservation of family, moral values and hence the society and, why not, also the preservation of our statehood.

I am sure that we shall not miss this unique opportunity of self-purification and that the future of the Armenian people will be built on the basis of united moral and material potential of all Armenians in the world.

Naira Melkoumian is Nagorno Karabagh Republic's Minister of Foreign Affairs. She has directly participated in the negotiation process for the settlement of the Karabagh conflict within the framework of the Minsk Group in the Organization for Security and Co-operation in Europe. A Doctor of Philology, she is the author of many publications. She has the diplomatic rank of Ambassador Extraordinary and Plenipotentiary.

Breast Cancer and Women's Primary Health Care

Rita Balian, moderator

The Creation of AAMUC in Armenia and its Implications

Rita Balian

It does not matter where we live or who we are, because the words "breast cancer" strike fear in all of us. Most of us have a personal story of someone—be it a family member or friend—who has been affected by breast cancer

Without public awareness, reliable screening, early detection and treatment or competent care, many women will die of cancer without even knowing that their cancer first started in their breast. Breast cancer has grown to alarming proportions throughout the world. In America, for example, the risk of developing breast cancer is one in every nine women. According to research, 180,200 new cases of breast cancer are developing each year. Nearly 45,000 are dying from the disease, and the risk is growing every year. The prediction is that within ten to fifteen years, between the years 2010 and 2015, one in every three women will be at risk for developing breast cancer in the United States. Armenia is no exception. According to the Ministry of Health of Armenia, "the leading cause of cancer deaths among women is breast cancer."

Surviving breast cancer is often determined by its early detection. The best way to detect breast cancer is through monthly self- examinations, annual mammograms, and annual medical exams. The value of mammography is that it identifies potential cancerous breast abnormalities, long before patients develop any physical symptoms. Early detection increases survival possibilities and treatment options.

Until April 1997, breast cancer detection in Armenia was inadequate. Armenia did not have any modern mammography equipment. The very few machines that were available were built in the 1960s. They were old, inaccurate, unreliable, and dangerous, producing intolerable levels of radiation. I was inspired to provide mammography screening to the women in Armenia because of personal circumstances. The lives of my two sisters in the United States were saved by the early detection of their breast cancer through mammography screening. Meanwhile, in Armenia, five of my good friends, who were mothers or grandmothers and distinguished members of their communities, lost their lives to cancer after finding out too late that their cancer had started in their breasts.

Therefore, as a response to the urgent need and request from Armenia for modern mammography equipment and pertinent knowledge, the Armenian American Cultural Association, Inc. (AACA), under my leadership in early 1996, initiated the Mammography Project for Armenia. After a year and a half of planning and preparation, The Armenian American Mammography University Center (AAMUC), a non-profit, state-of-the-art diagnostic facility in Yerevan, opened its doors to the public on April 28, 1997.

AAMUC's mission was and still is, "to save, prolong, and improve the lives of women in Armenia." AAMUC opened a new chapter in health care delivery for women in Armenia. AAMUC is located on the campus of the Yerevan State Medical University in downtown Yerevan. It is across from a metro station and is accessible to many women. It occupies 3,000 square feet of space. AAMUC provides high quality mammography and ultrasound screening, as well as public education regarding the importance of the early diagnosis of breast cancer. This is done through lectures, media, awareness campaigns, and the distribution of informational pamphlets.

Since 1997, the month of October in Armenia has been designated as "Breast Cancer Awareness Month," as it is in the United States. Every October, many activities are organized to educate the public, including, for example, medical missions to and from the United States, medical seminars, conferences, and regional lectures. These events culminate in the annual health walk through the streets of Yerevan. In 1999, the health walk attracted 3,000 participants, including four ambassadors with their spouses and staff, breast cancer survivors, advocates, medical students and residents, as well as 500 school children with their teachers. Funds raised from the health walk support the work of AAMUC.

Since opening in April 1997, nearly 15,000 women and twenty-five men have been screened at AAMUC. Among these, 200 have come from neighboring countries as far away as Uzbekistan.

Currently, AAMUC is averaging fifty patients a day. It sends to American-based AACA a monthly report detailing financial, operational, and statistical matters. Of the 15,000 women screened at AAMUC, 600 women, ranging in age from twenty-nine to seventy-five, have been diagnosed with breast cancer. Nearly 550 women have already received treatment in the form of surgery, chemotherapy, radiation, or a combination of these methods at the Oncology Hospital Center of Yerevan. In just three years, 550 families have received the "gift of hope," as well as an opportunity not to lose mothers, wives, or daughters to breast cancer. The children of these 550 families are grateful to all those who have donated their time and financial resources to this noble cause.

AAMUC made history in October 1999 in Armenia, when during our third medical mission, a stereo-tactic core biopsy table was installed and used on three patients. Such equipment does not exist anywhere else in the geographic region stretching from Central Europe to Japan, including the Middle East and Africa.

With this proven track record, AAMUC has earned the trust of the public as well as the respect of the medical community and the international organizations working in Armenia. Most important, the United States Embassy, the United States Agency for International Development (USAID), and the World Bank have repeatedly identified AAMUC as an example to many others because of its transparency, accountability, cost-effectiveness, and application of western administrative and management techniques. As such, AACA has received a grant from USAID to develop further its human resources; to establish a learning resource center with an on-line medical library at AAMUC; and to provide additional administrative assistance to AACA.

AAMUC's key features can be summarized as follows:

American state-of-the-art mammography and ultrasound equipment.

Well-trained and qualified staff of radiologists. Reliable medical screening provided to women.

Public awareness of the benefits of early detection of breast cancer.

Teaches value and technique of monthly breast self-examinations.

Encourages women to have regular mammography screening.

Distributes educational brochures in Eastern Armenian.

Referrals to qualified oncologists, surgeons, and pathologists.

Weekly meetings with specialists, surgeons/oncologists, and pathologists to discuss the conditions of cancer patients.

"Western" medical ethics and management practices exemplified.

On-going teaching resource at the Medical University of Armenia.

Replacing Soviet-era fear and suspicion of medical establishment with public confidence in good medical practices.

We are proud of our accomplishments so far, but we remain
acutely aware of how much more remains to be done. The establishment of AAMUC was only the first stage of our work for
women's health care in Armenia. For more than three years, we
realized the need to expand our services and introduce new
medical protocols. Therefore, AACA's two most important goals
are to expand the availability of mammography throughout
Armenia, and also to add more advanced diagnostic capabilities to verify the cancer and its stage.

It is vital to expand the availability of mammography, the
first goal, because the center cannot provide annual screening
to the 300,000 women over the age of thirty-five in Armenia. In
addition, many women cannot afford to travel to Yerevan. Therefore, there is a necessity for four additional satellite clinics to
open throughout Armenia.

The first such satellite clinic has been operating fully since
August 1, 2000. It is located in the northern suburb of Yerevan
in one of the largest women's hospitals. Between ten and fifteen
women are already being screened daily at this satellite clinic.
The second satellite clinic, located in the town of Gavar, is currently undergoing renovations and is scheduled to open in early
2001. This clinic will serve a population of 200,000. Research
indicates that the Lake Sevan region has the highest rate of breast
cancer—almost 20 percent. Our third and fourth satellite clinics
are planned for the earthquake zone in northern Armenia as
well as Goris in southern Armenia.

The second goal is to add advanced diagnostic capabilities.
Although mammography screening is the first step in determining the presence of breast cancer, sophisticated pathology services are necessary for diagnoses of suspicious masses. Therefore, AACA is planning to establish an in-house pathology lab

that will meet the center's breast cancer, and soon to be established cervical cancer, pathology needs.

From day one, AACA relied on the generosity of individuals and corporations from all over the United States and Canada. To date, over 600 individuals throughout North America have donated over $250,000. Private donations ranged from a five-dollar contribution, given by a great-grandmother residing in a nursing home, to two separate $30,000 donations from two family foundations.

While the sponsoring organization of AAMUC is American-based AACA, the parent organization in Armenia is the Women's Health Care Association (WHCA), a United Nations non-governmental organziation (NGO). Serving with me as co-president of WHCA is Dr. Hranoush Hakobyan. While Dr. Hakobyan oversees AAMUC's day-to-day operations in Armenia, I oversee development and long-term planning from the United States. Both of us volunteer our time and effort.

Dr. Hakobyan's presence at AAMUC inspires peace of mind in all of us. Without any fear of mismanagement or mediocre medical care, we are able to work tirelessly, in the United States, to provide for the needs of AAMUC. Dr. Hakobyan is regarded as one of the most honest people in Armenia, and her record proves her commitment to the welfare of Armenian women and children. The integrity of the mission and the quality of the care provided at AAMUC will never be compromised as long as we have this cooperation between us.

The Washington Hospital Center (WHC) has been a partner in our efforts from the very beginning. WHC is one of the largest hospitals in the United States and is nationally recognized for the superb quality of its medical care. Our medical advisory group is composed of prominent department heads and specialists from WHC. Its involvement in the project has been the backbone of our success, as they have guided us at every step. Dr. Ann Archer, who chairs the medical advisory group and has headed three medical missions to Armenia, stated that the medical quality of AAMUC rivals that of any American institution.

The doctors at AAMUC received their training from American specialists, during our first two medical missions. Additionally, two doctors were brought to the United States for two months of training at the Washington Hospital Center, Georgetown Medical Center and Walter Reed Medical Center. In July 2000, two additional radiologists will go to the United States for training. AAMUC, with its satellite clinic, retains five radiologists, three oncology and pathology consultants, three administrative assistants, two cleaning women, and one manager to provide first-class medical service to its patients. Additionally, through their salaries, AAMUC's employees are able to sustain the lives of their families.

AACA and AAMUC are guided by their joint motto: "Each time we save the life of a mother, we save the lives of her children, her family, and, thus, our nation." By working together we can save the lives of the mothers in Armenia; in so doing, we will not be obliged to build yet another orphanage.

Rita Balian avidly supports artistic, cultural, and humanitarian efforts. She was educated in psychology and education and has extensive business experience and an honorary doctorate from Yerevan State University. She is founding president of the Armenian-American Mammography University Center and co-president of the Women's Health Care Association.

The Position of Women in Primary Health Care

Ruzanna Yuzbashyan

My name is Ruzanna Yuzbashyan. I am honored to have the opportunity to speak at this conference of the Armenian International Women's Association not only because I'm taking part in a global event like this, but also because I'm speaking in front of women who have made every effort to support their compatriots' health issues regardless of the fact that they are not members of the medical profession. The women in Armenia acknowledge the enormous work their diasporan sisters did after the earthquake and during the years of cold and dark; they were with us and by our sides, traveling thousands of kilometers and overcoming many difficulties away from their warm and safe homes. Many of them are here now, in this hall. I can't mention all the names, as the list is too long. So, I will go on to my topic, to present the general features of our primary health care system and its people to you.

Review of the Primary Health Care System

A major portion of public health issues is connected with primary health care services that have always been available and accessible to the people. It is the primary level that associates with the person, family and community. It performs a pivotal function in the state health system and aims at meeting the

New Visions, New Horizons

basic medical and social requirements of the population by using simple and accessible medical technologies and by underlining the importance of early diagnostics and prophylaxis of disease.

Primary health care is provided through out-patient medical establishments (ambulatory clinics and polyclinics) such as:

- City polyclinics and dispensary
- Polyclinic section of medical institutions
- Regional Health Centers
- Regional Ambulatory Centers
- Regional Obstetric Posts

Out-patient clinics' health care functions are as follows:

- Early diagnostics and prophylaxis of the illnesses.
- Patients' treatment and follow-up observation, as well as hospitalization of patients requiring in-patient medical treatment, if necessary.
- Propagating a healthy mode of living and raising public awareness in this regard.

Given the general background of socio-economic conditions—the fall in living standards and restricted access to medi-

Medical Institutions Providing Primary Health Care									
	Polyclinics			Dental Clinics			Regional Health Centers	Regional Ambulatory Centers	Regional Obstetric Posts	In-Patient Clinics
	Adult	Child	Mixed	Adult	Child	Mixed				
1. Yerevan	28	10	6	10	5	0	0	0	0	46
2. Aragatsotn	0	0	4	0	0	1	16	1	89	5
3. Ararat	4	3	1	0	0	3	48	2	46	9
4. Armavir	2	2	3	2	2	0	41	7	37	11
5. Gegharkunik	4	4	1	0	0	4	23	1	59	8
6. Lori	6	6	4	2	1	2	18	10	86	24
7. Kotayk	3	3	2	0	0	3	27	4	31	7
8. Syunik	3	3	3	4	0	0	10	7	105	15
9. Vayots Dzor	0	0	3	0	0	0	1	4	36	6
10. Tavoush	3	3	1	0	0	1	10	7	40	11
11. Shirak	1	0	12	0	1	1	6	6	77	23
Total	54	34	40	20	9	14	204	49	606	165

cal services—people lost their faith and trust in the primary health care system despite its being the most accessible one.

Following the establishment of the paid medical system atten-
dance at polyclinics fell sharply.

Challenges Facing Women Working in the Primary Health Care System (Rights, Responsibilities Functions and Peculiarities of Work)

There are 16,930 women working in the primary health care
system, of whom 6,280 are physicians and 10,650 are nurses.
The overwhelming majority of specialists and administrative
workers (managers and deputies) in 423 outpatient medical institutions operating in the Republic of Armenia are women.

An enormous and very important job is being done in the
Regional Obstetric Posts bringing health care to the villages of
the republic. There are about 205 medical assistants, 136 mid-
wives and hundreds of nurses working in the medical posts of

	Medical Personnel							
	Physicians				Middle Medical Staff			
	District Therapist	District Pedia-tricians	Medical Special-ists	Total	Nurses	Medical Assistants	Obste-tricians	Total
1. Yerevan	2578	514	444	3536	3244	205	136	3389
2. Aragatsotn	46	36	118	200	670	5	68	743
3. Ararat	82	69	51	202	397	0	66	463
4. Armavir	112	96	114	322	572	25	73	670
5. Gegharkunik	79	71	55	205	690	19	54	763
6. Lori	107	96	393	596	1678	121	345	2144
7. Kotayk	79	75	345	499	1236	1	147	1384
8. Syunik	45	49	60	154	328	7	0	335
9. Vayots Dzor	12	17	23	52	158	2	18	178
10. Tavoush	48	48	79	175	372	7	42	421
11. Shirak	111	96	134	341	892	9	76	977
Total	3299	1167	1816	6282	10303	205	136	10644

this system. Sometimes, dozens of kilometers away from the
administrative center, where medical establishments with qualified personnel are situated, they selflessly perform their duties
day and night, often being underpaid. Imagine for a moment
the physicians and nurses of the ambulatory centers walking

from one village to another with vaccines in medical bags, vehicles being unavailable, to prevent the spread of disease.

Professionals in the primary health care system carry the responsibility for early detection and prevention of illnesses, especially that of tumors. In this sense, the establishment of the Armenian-American Mammography University Center is an invaluable gift to women. To raise women's consciousness in Armenia, to conduct health care awareness campaigns and to struggle against the growth of malignant tumors, especially breast cancer: these are the priorities of health care system's prophylactic programs.

We all want to preserve the nation's gene pool, improve the society's general health and contribute to its moral and psychological rehabilitation. Unfortunately, life is full of stresses. The distant echo of the devastating earthquake is felt even today. Stress factors accompany us in our everyday life. This results in a high frequency of the various diseases caused by stress. Therefore, spreading knowledge about health care to the society and conducting campaigns for healthy lifestyles will be among the priorities of the primary health care system along with the prevention of diseases. We hope to improve the doctor-patient relationship and solve all the family health care problems pointed out above by improving family medicine in the health care system.

Primary health care, like other parts of the health care system, requires considerable improvement. Structure, personnel, and training systems need change. We hope to build a health care system that operates at a level close to the standards of developed countries.

I know that we have a challenge to meet but there is one thing encouraging us: the majority of medical professionals are women, and we know women are persistent, purposeful and able to fight their way to the desired victory.

Women Doctors in the Workplace and at Home

A severe fate has fallen to Armenian women's lot at the end of the millennium. The present economic situation in Armenia dictates new relationships not common in Armenian history. If formerly the Armenian woman was mainly a pillar of the family, now she is a central figure in the workplace, too. In the workplace, the woman doctor takes responsibility for the patient's life, while the manager doctor takes also the responsibility for managing the whole work within the medical institution, administering economic and financial issues as well as the staff.

In Armenia, the first member of the medical profession one meets when having a health problem is a district doctor; abroad, one might consult an internist or a family doctor. In any case, the patient's health progress depends on that person's honesty, qualifications and experience. There are many challenges and obstacles along the way. Fundamental structural and educational changes, as well as changes in financing are already needed by the health system in our country. Undoubtedly, the major part of reforms will be directed to the primary health care system.

We realize that no reform can bring about significant progress, if the attitude of the society towards its own health status does not change and the qualification of the members of the medical profession does not improve.

The Role of Primary Health Care in Reproductive Health and Family Planning Issues

There is a widely held opinion that only women themselves should take care of their health. The reproductive health and family planning issues have been in the domain of gynecologists only; therefore men used to play a passive role in these matters. The primary health care specialists (family doctors and doctors in general practice) view these issues not only from the aspect of woman's health but also from the aspect of a family as a social unit. Hence, a big share of responsibilities will also be required of men.

The Role of Women in the Development of Public Health

The development of public health requires the significant participation of women. It is not a secret that in Armenian families women bear the main responsibility for educating the next generation. We have to educate future generations ready to take their share of responsibilities in the society, including the sphere of health.

I'm sure our visions for the future are full of confidence. Generations to come move toward new horizons guided by the caring hands of mothers and wives, now and forever, in all times and in all countries—the strong hands of Armenian women, who are the preservers of the nationality and the keepers of traditions.

Ruzanna Yuzbashyan, M.D., heads the Primary Health Care Department of the Ministry of Health in Armenia, and teaches at Yerevan State Medical University. Previously Deputy Director of Polyclinic #19 in Yerevan, she is a member of the Working Group on Developing a Family Medicine Program in Armenia.

WOMEN'S RIGHTS

Lala Petrosian, moderator

The Problem of Women's Equality in Armenia

Gohar Matinian and Liana Hakobyan

The problem of equality between men and women can be discussed in two aspects—*de jure* and *de facto*.

The existence of *de jure* equality in the Republic of Armenia is indisputable. All the legal guarantees for gender equality are present. There are no discriminatory legal norms or provisions in the legislation of the Republic.

But the existence of *de jure* equality does not guarantee real equality, and it is indisputable that a gap exists between *de jure* and *de facto* equality in our country. To demonstrate this, it is sufficient to cite the following: The United Nations Convention on the Elimination of All Forms of Discrimination Against Women was one of the first international legal instruments ratified by the Republic of Armenia. Through this ratification the government's obligation to ensure real equality between men and women was raised to the level of an international obligation. But evidence of the fact that the obligation has not yet been fulfilled can be cited: In 1997 an Armenian delegation presented the national report on implementation of the Convention's provisions in our Republic to the United Nations Commission on the Elimination of Discrimination Against Women. There was not a single female representative; on the contrary, the delegation consisted of male representatives only. It is significant that the Republic of Armenia was the only one among the eight states presenting their national reports at this session which had such a structure of delegates.

The most obvious expression of the absence of real equality between men and women is the very limited representation of Armenian women in the highest bodies of public authority.

What are the factors that limit Armenian women's active participation in the decision-making process and their representation in the highest bodies of public authority?

1. The first limiting factor can be found in the firm stereotypes of men's and women's roles in our society, according to which the women's role is connected with the household and family obligations and women's intellectual and working abilities are underestimated.

2. The second reason for women's passive participation in the sphere of public administration, which is more serious, is that female abilities are underestimated not only by males, but also by women themselves. Many women consider that the qualities required for high positions in the sphere of public administration are inconsistent with a woman's nature. Women's prejudices concerning their social role naturally form internal restraints, and, as a result, many women who have the skills required to hold responsible positions in high levels of public administration are reluctant to participate in public affairs.

3. Another reason is that family responsibilities are shared between men and women unfairly. The main burden in the family is laid upon women, a situation which limits their potential to find the time and develop the skills required for participation in decision-making in wider public forums.

Today, in many countries, in order to ensure women's active representation in state bodies, a quota system is used. This means that a certain set number of seats are ensured for women in parliaments by virtue of law. But recently in some countries where this system is used a question is raised: "Is the application of a quota system consistent with the principle of men's and women's equality?" This question has taken an interesting course in Switzerland. The federal court of that country has reviewed a draft law which, in order to ensure sufficient representation of women in the government, determined that the number of women in the legislative, executive, and judicial bodies of each canton must be proportionate to the number of males and females populating the canton. The federal court ruled that the draft law, whose aim was to ensure constant seats for women in three branches of the state power through this mechanism, was contrary to its major principles. The Court reasoned its decision on the following ground: According to Article 4.2 of the Swiss Constitution, men and women are equal before the law; legislation ensures their equality in the sphere of education, in the family, and in labor relations. The purpose of the draft law was the improvement of women's opportunities, a goal which however is inconsistent with the principle of the equality of men and women. In order to improve women's opportunities, other measures can be taken. Besides, the federal court found that the draft law was not only inconsistent with the principle of gender equality, but it also represented a violation of universal and equal electoral rights. The voters would be deprived of the opportunity for free election.

The quota system was tried also in our republic in order to ensure constant seats for women in the National Assembly by the adoption of the new Electoral Code. According to Article 100, "Women shall constitute at least 5 percent of the candidates in the electoral lists presented by a party for the elections to the National Assembly by the proportional system." But the 1999 elections indicated that this provision did not achieve its aim, because the names of women were at the end of the electoral lists. As a result of these elections, the National Assembly now has only four women members instead of the twelve women members of the former parliament.

Thus, in order to ensure real equality between men and women and to encourage women's active participation in political life, it is necessary first of all to overcome women's own internal prejudices in order to achieve true liberty. Second, it is necessary to take measures to eliminate the established stereotypes regarding men's and women's roles in society. Finally, in order to ensure sufficient representation by women in the institutions of state authority, it may be advisable to use quota systems.

Gohar Matinian is Judge of the Appellate Court on Civil Cases of the Republic of Armenia. Liana Hakobyan is Assistant Judge of the Constitutional Court of the Republic of Armenia.

ARTS

Lois Melkonian, moderator

Armenian Women of the Stage

Alice Navasargian

Of my many reasons for writing on this subject, my main one is to memorialize the important role of Armenian women in the history of art in our culture for future generations of Armenians.

I wrote my book, *Armenian Women of the Stage* (1999), not only in the hope of preserving and appreciating an important aspect of Armenian culture, but also for the establishment of my own patriotic self-consciousness, my dignity, and my pride as an Armenian. This book is not just a collection of biographies and beautiful photographs, but is also a chronicle of the dramatic renaissance of Armenian culture in the nineteenth and twentieth centuries.

It is a history of stage performance, with the biographies of some very brave, talented, and determined Armenian women who performed on the world stage. It is about amazing stage heroines who fought for their national recognition and freedom, human dignity, and creativity—each in her unique manner. For the Armenian woman, marriage, motherhood, and the love of her family make the pursuit of a meaningful career extremely difficult. These women deserve immense praise and recognition for achieving top positions in the world of arts, drama, and music.

It is the women of Armenian descent who are mainly responsible for the continued growth and flourishing of our culture. We raise children who speak our tongue, listen to our music, and appreciate our history. So it is not a coincidence that we say *Mayr hayrenik, Mayreni lezoo, Mayreni barbar,* and we call the symbol of all Armenians and Armenia *"Mayr Hayastan."* What makes the women in my study so exceptional is that they managed to fill their rôles as matriarchs while also tapping their creative energies in brilliant performances on the worl stage. It is in this light that Armenian women of the stage should be remembered. I hope readers of the biographies of these artists can feel in their own souls and life experiences each success and difficulty, each achievement and misfortune, each moment of happiness and tragedy. Theirs was not an easy task. Every time they stepped on the stage to perform, they were representing us Armenians. Without doubt these brave women did a tremendous and excellent job.

Work cited:

Navasargian, Alice. 1999. *Armenian Women of the Stage.* Glendale, CA: TriA

Alice Navasargian was born in Tabriz, Iran, where she studied art and music for many years. She received her bachelor's degree in Armenology from the University of Tehran. Since coming to the United States, she has written and published two books: *Iran-Armenia: Golden Bridges,* which presents artworks and biographies of 55 Iranian-born Armenian painters, and *Armenian Women of the Stage,* in which she introduces 63 Armenian women in the performing arts, from the mid-nineteenth century to the present day.

My Uncle Bill

Jacqueline Papazian Kazarian

"In the time of your life, live...so that in that good there shall be no ugliness or death for yourself, or any life your life touches. Seek goodness everywhere."—The Time of Your Life 1940

"Take it as it comes, soon enough the past, the present and the future will be the time it is."—Not Dying 1963

I have traveled halfway around the world to add another dimension to the legacy of William Saroyan, my Uncle Bill. I watched him soar to fame and later in life I saw him retreat to obscurity. He was my Uncle Bill before he became the famous "Daring Young Man."

The early years tell much about things he valued: family, children, home and love. He impacted my life in many ways. I was the second of the five Papazian children. Takhooi, my grandmother, Uncle Bill and Aunt Cosette (the eldest of the four Saroyan children) lived within walking distance of our home in San Francisco. Daily visits back and forth were a part of each day. Our world was family, and Uncle Bill was the appointed babysitter on Saturday mornings, especially to my older sister Gloria and me. Often, he would take us to Golden Gate Park, which was down the hill from his upper flat at 348 Carl Street. The building is still there, overlooking Kezar Stadium.

Uncle Bill was nineteen years old when I was born. He was energetic, fun, creative and he loved us. If one of us was in a school play and he was away, he made it home for the opening performance. He would sit in the first row and clap the loudest. If there was any reason for laughter, his Saroyan laugh was heard above the others. He did not have favorites; he was fair and uncritical. If my sister and I had a silly fight while we were in the playground, he would say, "Okay kids, if you can't get along, we're going home." Sometimes it straightened us out, sometimes not.

The stories that follow, like indelible ink, are permanently etched in my mind. They were life changing for me. My mother had five children in ten years and little time to spend playing or entertaining us. Uncle Bill, Nana (my grandmother) and Cosette loved doing that part and it helped mother.

The first story takes place when I was around six years old.  It happened in the Spring, on a bright, clear Saturday morning. Uncle Bill had a plan but he chose to begin each morning in an open, democratic way "Who wants to...?" and before he had finished, I would eagerly shout, "I do!" He would burst into his loud, riotous, Saroyan laugh and say "Jackie, I haven't finished yet, hold it." The question that day "Who wants to go for a walk?" Uncle Bill often walked several miles to town. Town for him was downtown San Francisco. This walk was to the Pacific Ocean through Golden Gate Park. Even though the walk was long, I felt that I was in some fairyland with my Uncle giving us a nature lesson. Each tree, flower, animal, bird, rock, or stream became a reason to stop, look and explore. He had an explanation for each, and I found it sheer enchantment. I still love to walk.

The next episode is about learning. I was a student in Jefferson Grammar School; I hated to read and my grades confirmed it. My sister, glorious Gloria, didn't read books, she devoured them. If you couldn't find her, she was probably hiding, reading a book. She excelled in school and won every reading contest in the library. She and I visited the public library every week and she would leave with a stack of books. I would wander through the library quietly, taking books off the shelf with no intention of taking any home. I was there because of my big sister. She was two and a half years older and she wouldn't let me forget it. I was close to failing reading. My mother was sent a note from my teacher informing her that I would be kept after school for a Remedial Reading Class. Distressed about it, I went to Uncle Bill. He knew Gloria was the family reader with a straight 'A' report card and he knew of my lack of interest in reading. Discouraged, I asked him, "Uncle Bill, is it so bad that I don't like to read?" He sensed my unhappiness and said "Jackie, when you understand the importance of reading and you want to learn to read, you will." His words gave me hope. A few months later my mother was called to school to meet with my teacher. There were only three of us: Miss Finney, Mother and me.

Miss Finney said to my mother "Mrs. Papazian, I don't know how to explain it, but Jacqueline has had a change in attitude. She wants to read and is now the best in the Remedial Class. Her progress has been quite amazing. I am so pleased with her progress." I began to cry. Mother and I walked home. She held my hand and I was happy with my new victory at school.

I am sure that someone in this audience will relate to this next experience. It is pretty safe to say that every little girl has at least one bad habit. I had a few. I was sassy and nosey but worst of all, I bit my nails. My mother wasn't happy about it and actually took me to the doctor, who assured her that he had the situation under control. He said, "Just put iodine on her fingers and she will not bite them." Mother followed his orders. The taste was awful but I continued.

The year was 1935. I was seven and a half; family picnics were the ideal Sunday outing for five children who needed plenty of space to run, play and shout. Mother would pack a great picnic and off we would go. By Monday, we were ready for the structure of school and its formal demands. My reward for such holidays was a dose of painful, itchy, poison oak, which kept me home from school for days on end. My face became swollen and my eyes nearly shut. I spent most of the time in my bedroom with the shade down feeling ugly and forsaken. An occasional friend would come to visit and invariably say, "Jackie you look horrible, I hardly recognize you." I would cringe inside. I finally called my mother and said, "I don't want anyone to visit me!"

One afternoon, Uncle Bill called mother to say he was stopping by. I was still in my bedroom feeling awful. He came in, sat on the edge of my bed, looked at me in silence... What could he say? He gently picked up my hand. It was the only thing not covered with poison oak. Finally he said, "Jackie, your little hands are beautiful and your fingers are long and pretty." He didn't mention a word about my nails or how ugly I looked. He put my hand down and left the room.

I never bit my nails again.

The next story happened nineteen years later, in 1954. I was twenty-four, not in love and not engaged. Uncle Bill was living in his new home in the Colony, in Malibu. His beach house was built on piles. When the tide was in, the waves would crash under the house. It took time to get used to the waves and the first night I was afraid I would end up somewhere in the Pacific. He assured me that I was fine and that I would get used to the rhythm of the ocean. I was there to save him from the heat and glaring sun that beat into every room. Each room had huge floor to ceiling windows that made the ocean a wall of the house.

He would sit at a card table in front of the window, with Chopin, Bach or some other piano recording playing and he would type away for hours, hardly moving, never saying a word. I knew he was a writer but I had never seen him in action, like this, such concentration. The words and thoughts swiftly flew on to the paper. I was amazed. The typewriter made a continuous, rhythmic tapping sound. We had a schedule and he had a daily work plan. We would get up early in the morning, have black coffee, cheese, fruit and bread and then we would talk. Whenever he wanted to get to work he would simply announce "I've got to get back to work now." I would disappear into my room to work on the draperies for the beach house, which was the reason why I was there.

When he finished for the day we would go shopping in the Village and, after lunch or dinner, we would resume our conversation. It was on one of these occasions that I dared to ask him about finding Mr. Right. I trusted him to tell me the truth. He had never failed me. I was taken back by his answer. "Jackie," he said, "You have it all wrong. You don't even think about finding Mr. Right. You must continue to grow and learn, working from the inside out, understanding yourself and becoming the best you can be. When that happens, Mr. Right will turn up. There is to be no looking." I was satisfied but he didn't stop there. "You must be aware of packaging. Think of yourself as a gift. If you want to look like something from the five and ten cent store, you package yourself like that. If you want to look like something from Tiffany's, you package yourself like that. It is all about packaging and timing." He stopped and then began again: "The most important thing is what I will now tell you, so listen carefully and remember." I was sitting on the edge of the chair lost in his words. "Jackie," he said, "at best, and with everything in your favor (same ethnic background, education, socio economic status, and religion), your decision to marry will be the most demanding, challenging and critical decision you will make in your life. So make it carefully!" I went to my room and wrote what he told me on a piece of paper. I still have that piece of paper tucked inside my Bible.

Love, family, and children were at the very heart of Uncle Bill's being and he wrote much about each. (*Jim Dandy*, the play. The novels: *The Human Comedy; Papa You're Crazy; Mama I Love You*). The role of father was most important to him and his hundreds of letters to his children and his desire to be a part of their lives was a dream he was not able to realize.

My final thoughts and comments have never been mentioned in spite of the fact that his words are often quoted and remembered. My Uncle Bill was enlightened, his words were prophetic. Please think of Matthew 18:19, "If two of you shall agree"… and then consider the 1935 story, "The Armenian & the Armenian." He wrote, "See if they will not live again when two of them meet…"

Armenia became a nation in 1991. Who would have thought it possible? The great Armenian-American writer Saroyan did at a time when such an idea was preposterous. My Uncle Bill left a legacy for Armenians to live by and he drew upon the human experience to uncover basic needs and cries of humanity.

Love one another.

Armenia will prevail, humanity will survive.

You wait and see!

Read his work. Talk about his writing.

AIWA women—let us be proud of our great culture, our God given rôle and our motherland, Armenia.

"In the time of your life, live…"

He would want it that way and so do I.

Works cited:

Saroyan, William

1940   *The Time of Your Life*. In: *Three Plays: My Heart's in the Highlands, The Time of Your Life, Love's Old Sweet Song*. New York: Harcourt, Brace and Company.

1943   *The Human Comedy*. New York: Harcourt, Brace and Company.

1947 *Jim Dandy, Fat Man in a Famine; A Play.* New York: Harcourt, Brace and Company.

1956 *Mama, I Love You.* Boston: Little, Brown.

1957 *Papa, You're Crazy.* Boston: Little, Brown.

1963 *Not Dying.* New York: Harcourt, Brace & World.

Jacqueline Papazian Kazarian is a niece of author/playwright William Saroyan. She is the Executive Director of the William Saroyan Literary Foundation International, based in San Francisco. She is also a health educator and a distinguished toastmaster.

Reflected Glory: Using the Arts to Accomplish Broader Goals

Laurel Karabian

As we meet in this historic building on Republic Square, I am reminded of the early the days of another republic. In 1780, while attending the Continental Congress, John Adams wrote to his wife Abigail, "I must study politics and war, that my sons may have liberty to study mathematics and philosophy, commerce and agriculture in order to give their children a right to study painting, poetry, music [and] architecture."

When the wave of post-Genocide immigrants settled into their adopted countries, they wasted little time bringing an appreciation of creativity back into their lives. They had negotiated their new environments, working hard to endow their offspring with renewed educational and economic security. Theatrical societies, art exhibits, musicales and recitations were natural outlets for these survivors.

Today, the world increasingly recognizes the disparate complexities of various ethnicities. Diversity was the watch word that closed out the twentieth century and we can take advantage of this interest with strategies to develop greater cultural and political awareness of Armenia and Armenians through the arts. Our goal is focused on achieving recognition for our creative geniuses not as "great Armenian artists," but as "great artists," known for their work, not their nationality, just as Picasso, who happens to be Spanish, Sibelius who happens to be Finnish, or James Joyce who happens to be Irish are known first for their masterpieces, and then for the glory they reflect back to the heritage that inspired them.

In recent years, we have witnessed an expansion in the way that art by Armenians is presented. No longer content with appreciative audiences made up of ourselves, we are seeking ways to reach the world whose names don't end with "ian."

However, these efforts to secure broader forums rarely succeed unless we enlist the strength of established organizations with built-in audience bases. With competition from so many angles, we can't afford to take a "Field of Dreams" attitude. Too often we make the fatal error of naively assuming that the techniques we use to promote events to ourselves will be equally appealing to a broader market.

A number of years ago, I attended a meeting regarding the American tour of a major Armenian cultural organization. It was shortly after the breakup of the Soviet Union, and the Los Angeles organizers were certain that after that monumental change in global geography, the event would garner inordinate attention throughout Southern California and would provide a desirable positive boost in the level of recognition Armenia achieves as a sophisticated nation. Included in the tour roster were several artists who also had ties to Iran, Russia and Egypt, so when references were made to promoting the event in the "odar" press, I thought we were talking about newspapers and television stations directed at those ethnic groups. Ten minutes later I realized that the passing reference to the odar press meant the Los Angeles Times. At the very time we want to be "in," we can't be naming others the outsiders. Such slips as these betray a fundamental misunderstanding of the concept of working from within to accomplish our purpose.

When Parajanov films were included in the Rotterdam Film Festival, alongside those of Martin Scorsese, Eric Rohmer and David Lynch; when our Illuminated Manuscripts were included in exhibits at the J. P. Morgan Library in New York or the Getty Museum in Malibu; when our treasures were on display at the Vatican Museum and when Armenia had pavilions at the past three Venice Biennales, we paid attention—and so did the rest of the world. These are tremendous opportunities for political as well as cultural advantage.

Years ago the Center Theatre Group, Southern California's largest and most important theatre company, began an outreach project to serve Los Angeles's various ethnic groups. Season by season, plays were staged addressing Hispanic, Black, Jewish, Japanese and Vietnamese issues. Recognizing the strength and number of Armenians in Los Angeles, a search was initiated for an appropriate piece, resulting in Leslie Ayvazian's "Nine Armenians." Aside from the dialogue on stage, the experience included articles about Armenia and the Armenians in California, interviews with the playwright and actors, and the palpable sense that Armenians are an acknowledged entity in the framework of Southern California life. The Center Theatre Group needed us to demonstrate another dimension to its commitment to multiculturalism and to tap into our ticket buyers, but we benefited from the exposure to their audiences as well.

Multiculturalism is a concept that has been nearly "buzzed" to death. Arenas catering to widespread audiences are not going to come looking for us. Instead, we must concentrate on guerrilla engagement of appropriate venues that will bring works by composers, dramatists, visual artists, dance makers, writers and so on, to mainstream cultural institutions. Through these associations we have the opportunity not only to support the creative expressions of our artists, but also to focus attention on the traditions and ancestry from which they stem. At the same time that our concerns lie with protecting the political integrity of our Republic and the economic stability and physical needs of is people, we cannot abandon to future generations the obligation to protects its soul.

I would like to share with you a project that I am involved with in San Francisco, namely the presentation of Dickran Chukhadjian's Opera *Arshak II* in September, 2001. This production was in the works for about five years and was scheduled to culminate with six performances on the subscription season. 20,000 American opera afficionados were to hear a work by an Armenian composer, conducted by an Armenian, sung in Armenian by a number of Armenian virtuosi, mounted by the largest American company outside of New York. The public relations value for us is enormous. Publicity materials and program books contain contextual expositions and historical perspectives. School children and seniors attend special performances. Millions of commercial impressions appear in print, radio and television media. In a town as artsy as San Francisco it is hard to avoid extensive publicity, ads, articles and interviews designed to enhance the awareness of the opera and its origins. The interest surrounding the restoration of a previously unheard work by a composer whose greatness we acknowledge, but who is all but unknown in the west also extends to opera circles beyond the Bay Area—to cities such as Detroit, Los Angeles and Washington, D.C. The ultimate goal of adding an Armenian opera to the occidental repertoire is yet to be reached.

This project has not been without controversy. The San Francisco Opera was to present a restoration of the original 1868 edition, translated into Armenian. The story line is dramatic and tragic and not intended to be a history lesson. It is an opera. The text is a vehicle for the music, and the whole production is a vehicle to show off one of our great musical treasures while increasing general respect for our culture adding a bit of depth to what is generally known about us. At a time when most general public perceptions of Armenia and Armenians is based on news stories of wars, assassinations and gang conflicts, shouldn't we have a few positive sound bites?

Laurel Karabian, a graduate of Pomona College and UCLA, was the first president of AIWA's Los Angeles affiliate. In development for the Los Angeles Philharmonic prior to consulting for non-profit organizations, including the Armenian Library and Museum of America, San Francisco Opera's *Arshak II,* and the California Arts Council, she is currently Los Angeles County Art Commissioner and on the Board of Directors of the Pepperdine University Center for the Arts.

CHANGES IN FAMILY STRUCTURE

Nazenik Sargsyan, moderator

The Role of Women in Contemporary Society

Mariam Torosyan

In the course of history, Armenian women had no rights. Historical sources testify to that.

In the past, mothers would be deprived of their rights to bring up their children when they divorced. Women were responsible only for things that had to do with their role in the family, such as giving birth to children, raising them and managing the household.

Women's conditions changed only in the 20th century. Due to scientific progress and technological advance the position of a woman changed in the whole world, particularly, in Armenia. Full involvement in the country's social and political life enabled women to contribute to all activities of social life.

During the last decade, dozens of women's organizations, committees and relief funds have been established. The activities of these Non-Governmental Organizations contribute to the democratization process, enhancement of women's status, provision of equal rights and equal opportunities for men and women in Armenia, and the study of key issues that emerged during recent years.

Many problematic processes of the transition out of the Soviet Union were accompanied by undesirable demographic shifts in Armenia. Both the marriage rate and birth rates have dropped.

The average age of those getting married is 23. The absolute rate of yearly births has decreased by half.

We are next to last on the list of Central and East European countries by level of female employment. Women account for 71.5 percent of the total number of unemployed registered in Armenia. The number of women working in the so-called "feminine" spheres such as education, culture, health, and social services has declined every year. Parallel to the objective reasons there are the subjective ones, particularly the conventions of the workplace. The criteria for assessing professional experience very often express the talents and interests of men, while talents and interests of women are not considered. These conventions match the traditions that have existed in our society since ancient times; a woman in Armenia never engaged in public relations. This stereotype has not yet broken down. It is confirmed by the fact that very few women are involved in politics and hold leading posts. It cannot be explained simply by the absence of enthusiasm in our women, who face diverse social and economic challenges. It is a result of a patriarchal and conservative view of women. The position of mother, reserved for women by nature, is viewed as primary and profoundly important. Our women have always fulfilled their duties in an excellent way and can serve as an example for many others.

Today Armenian women are not only impelled to shoulder the heavy burden of keeping the family, but are forced to become the breadwinners due to male emigration. Shouldering double responsibility, the women find themselves in an extremely difficult situation as the children almost run out of control.

We all know the father's role is essential in educating the children, especially the boys. As a result of being continuously surrounded by women (by the mother at home, by the teachers at school), a certain mode of behavior (it is being investigated by psychologists) is developed in boys. The absence of the father gives rise to a sense of inferiority and a feeling of insecurity. The children become less sociable and more vulnerable. Growing up without a father may have negative consequences tomorrow. We may face a problem of feminization of a certain part of growing generation. We must see the reality clearly and distinctly; with foresight we can avoid the possible undesirable consequences.

Another fact causing a particular concern and anxiety is the emigration of men and their prolonged stays abroad. It results in men starting up a second family abroad and leads to the breaking of contacts with the official family, thus causing the family to fall apart. So, a stressful situation, a terrible and unavoidable threat, is added on to the difficult social conditions existing in the family.

These problems require a thorough investigation to reveal the whole spectrum of negative after-effects of these processes. Our sociologists and psychologists should express their opinion in this regard.

Speaking of discrimination against women, it should be noted that an understanding of age qualification has emerged recently. Certain age limitations may be reasonable in the service sector when physical capacity is required. For example some physically demanding jobs may be restricted to the 18-30 year old age group. These jobs here require strength and agility; only the young ones are able to cope with this load. This doesn't cause worry. Worry is aroused by the fact that this phenomenon is gradually spreading to other spheres, thus hindering the entrance of highly qualified specialists into these spheres. Women's high intellectual abilities are being ignored: women account for 56 percent of those with higher education, and in spheres like education, culture and health about 60-80 percent are women.

In Armenia, the value of intellectual work is underestimated so much that a woman with higher education has to be engaged in small-scale commerce, do clerical work or some other job not related to her educational level. We must understand how the use of age qualifications breaks the principle of social justice by excluding women from creative or scientific work. The feeling of being ignored thus appears as an unavoidable fact and destroys women's desire to develop and advance their intellectual abilities.

Women's lives revolve around their children. The children's fates and futures are of profound importance to them. I've conducted a survey among students to find out the opinion of young men regarding the issue of securing a job after graduating from an institution of higher education. When asked, "What are you going to do, if you fail to get a job after graduation?" Seventy-eight percent of respondents said that they would be obliged to look for a job outside the Republic of Armenia. Though this survey included a small group of people (only seventy persons), it raises concerns and is not optimistic. It is nonsense to think there is even one Armenian mother who would like her child to leave the homeland in search of work.

Armenian women carry the unbearable burden of all the difficulties and troubles of the last decade on their shoulders in these hard times—the cold, starvation, blockade, earthquake, and war in Artsakh. Today they are uniting with their diasporan sisters in order to walk jointly, hand in hand, in search of solutions to the current problems. Today we have not gathered here by chance. In these years of suffering, the call of historic reminiscences of the Armenian people awakens and appeals for unity in the name of prosperity and well being of the fatherland.

Mariam Torosyan has been a music teacher and a choral conductor for many years. She is a graduate of the Armenian Pedagogical Institute Department of Music. She is interested in folk art, fine art, and theater music.

WOMEN'S PSYCHOLOGICAL AND SPIRITUAL HEALTH

Seda Ebrahimi-Keshishian, moderator

Armenian Society in Transition; Effects on the Family

Karine Nalchajyan

Socio-economic and political changes and shake-ups taking place in Armenia during the last ten years have significantly changed the socio-psychological situation in the country. The individual and the whole society came out of their stable state of private and public life and are still in the process of structural and functional formation.

What were those changes? How did the adaptation of the society living in a progressing economic crisis proceed? What are the characteristic features of various stresses acquired in that process?

We propose the hypothesis that a transition from a totalitarian to a civil society logically results in changes in both social and gender roles and status, which are expressed as extreme social polarization and have given birth to a great number of stress factors.

Disintegration of the economy was rapid and in no time unemployment overwhelmed both the male and female parts of the population.

To assess the power of that blow for a woman, it is enough to state the fact, that in the post-Soviet period the percentage of women among technical specialists with higher education was higher than that of men.

Therefore, it is natural that self-assertion via economic activity of an Armenian woman with higher education is of vital importance. Moreover, observations demonstrate that Armenian women see economic activity as one of the basic pleasures in life. For women this is both self-assertion and self-expression.

It is noteworthy that, as the observations testify, middle-aged women are more inclined to live in cozy living conditions created by their husbands. If the desire of younger women for the economic activity from a psychological viewpoint is explained by the acquirement of stable self-esteem, women over 50 years of age probably have a conviction derived from their life experience that employment and financial independence are important prerequisites for psychological comfortable state and stable individuality.

The society passing through this acute and many-faceted crisis of transition is undoubtedly a society exposed to stress. Strong and continuous stress destroys a person's mental and physical health and causes aggression and exasperation in relations with other people. Changes in social life unavoidably put the members of that society under stress. In such conditions stress factors cannot but enter the family and make family life vulnerable. The family living in a crisis-ridden society is not always able to withstand the inner crisis and to grapple with it easily.

First of all, we should state that during the last decade the overwhelming majority of stressors affecting Armenian society were of a distress nature. That is, they were connected with unpleasant overstrains: general unemployment, impoverishment, cold darkness, extreme social polarization, and war. The list can be continued. Not to sin against the truth we should also record the stressors having a eustress (connected with pleasant strains) nature: military successes, transparency of borders, awakening of national self-consciousness, noble eruption of national feelings (especially at the end of the 1980s), opportunity for civil activity, and freedom of speech.

Nevertheless, the collapse was so dizzying that the circumstances mentioned last were either not perceived in all their acuteness or even depreciated in that maelstrom. Social consciousness underwent deep and irretrievable shifts.

The massive army of stressors noisily entered the lives of each and every person, entered the families and marked the spiritual lives of people causing radical transformations. Social and political shake-ups and convulsions became personalized and each individual felt a great impact.

The typical, unavoidable stressors of everyday life—unpleasant everyday events, domestic affairs, housekeeping duties, conflicts within the family and at work— abruptly escalated, turning the normal tension of life into a contest for survival, torturing and depressing. Procurement of daily bread became a major issue. The society that had a high education level, and where cultural demands formerly played a considerable role, suddenly found itself in a chasm of pressing material-oriented demands only. Moreover, it happened immediately after the awakening of national self-consciousness—an enhanced self-expression from a spiritual and moral point of view.

This decline, having proceeded on the background of total disappointment, directly affected the moral character of people. Disappointment with the leaders having come to power by making use of love and trust of the whole people was a powerful stress.

The overwhelming majority of the society members were in a spiritual crisis, and socio-psychological adaptation to the new conditions was extremely difficult. These adaptation difficulties made people quarrelsome, discontented, aggressive and egoistic.

Each person focused on the survival of his family and himself. The family became the only place where a disappointed person could feel psychologically secure. But inner family relations underwent significant shifts, too. Being unable to support the family, which was traditionally regarded as a male affair, the spouses became discouraged. Due to this shift in the emotional life of men, a sense of guilt towards the family and children became dominant. Psychologists know that a strongly expressed sense of guilt testifies to the person's serious internal conflict and even neuroticism. Weakening of the man's role in the family gave birth to diverse inner contradictions in the psychology of the woman. Waste of mental and physical strength and desperation resulted in the paralysis of the physical and mental strengths of the society.

Another cause for stress in family life is the education crisis. The fact is that education and knowledge have always been of the utmost value to Armenian society. Even under the burden of material difficulties the education of the children is still an essential spiritual requirement for every Armenian. On one hand, education continues to remain a spiritual demand; on the other hand, there is an anxiety about the ability to meet that demand. So, poor life-conditions from this point of view have disturbed the family peace.

Another urgent problem for the Armenian family living in Armenia today is emigration, when the male family members leave the country in search of work. Surveys show that women prefer having their husbands by their sides, rather than having material security. Armenian women barely endure the emigration of their husbands.

And so, deep social, economic and political processes taking place in Armenia during the last ten years have been directly reflected in the family. Traditionally treated by Armenians as the primary small social group, the family withstands these forces in a weakened emotional state.

Karine Nalchajyan, Ph.D., graduate of Yerevan State University and Institute, is docent to psychology chair of the State Institute of Foreign Languages. She is a psychologist at the Children's Early Socialization French-Armenian Center and head of the NGO Makhutjun, Scientific, Practical, and Analytical Center of Psychological Research.

Women and Caregiving: Alzheimer's Disease and Related Disorders

Leilani Doty

Alzheimer's disease and related dementias are especially critical issues for women for two main reasons. First, more women than men are diagnosed with Alzheimer's disease. Second, typically the family caregiver is the wife because she lives closest to (usually with) the patient and is most available for help.

Strong cultural traditions have established women as the predominant caregivers in Armenian and diaspora families even when women have multiple responsibilities within the family unit in professional or leadership roles. The challenges of multiple demands, especially those of care giving for family members needing special attention and health care for decades, may tax the health of the woman caregiver as well as the extended family. This paper overviews three major relevant issues: 1) the importance of early medical evaluation and intervention, 2) planning ahead for long-term care, and 3) accessing care partners and resources.

Memory Changes with Aging

Memory allows people to learn and benefit from past experiences. Typically, memory ability slows down with aging but may be lost when there is pathology or disease. For example, while a teenager can quickly store and recall information, by the mid-thirties, a person must have meaning and value in the new information and rehearse it for good memory. After the age of seventy-five, slower body function results in slower learning, decision-making and recall. Changes in circulation, malnutrition or diseases that affect the brain can interfere with its function and thus with memory.

Changes in short-term memory versus changes in long-term memory serve as warnings about brain cell health. Though about one hundred billion neurons exist in the brain, plus many other cells—including astrocytes and stem cells that support the neurons—physical changes such as arteriosclerosis may impede the function of neuron and nerve chemicals (neurotransmitters) and result in the transmission of partial or no messages. Thus, a person may be unable to remember or do other thinking (cognitive) activities such as math or talking.

Dementia

Dementia is the decline of mental abilities. The decline may involve memory, knowledge, decision-making skills, communication or change in ability to do daily chores such as driving the car or cooking. Personality may change. People with dementia may struggle with tasks that were once easy. They may forget names, if they just ate breakfast, or the way home from the market. When a person suffers from short-term memory loss, forgets the names of people or objects, struggles with routine tasks or simple decisions, a careful medical evaluation with a series of tests will determine if, of the more than one hundred dementias, the health change is treatable (reversible), may be slowed down (vascular dementias), or is progressive (Alzheimer's disease).

Treatable or Reversible Memory Disorders and Dementias

Ten to fifteen percent of memory disorders are treatable or reversible if caught early enough. When changes in thyroid balance, a vitamin deficiency, improper medication, stress, depression, anxiety, or related conditions receive medical treatment, the person may regain healthy brain function. Neglect of such conditions may result in severe dysfunction resembling Alzheimer's disease.

In Armenia, recent reports of inadequate nutrition in youth resulting from iodine deficiency, a few decades later may lead to thyroid disorders such as hypothyroidism or hyperthyroidism that may look like Alzheimer's disease. Vitamin B (B1, B6, B12, folate and niacin) deficiencies may result in a number of nerve system problems such as losing sensation or control in the feet and hands as well as memory and thinking problems. The stress of Armenians during the recent decade (and perhaps the past several decades) of boundary wars, earthquakes, and drought may lead to frontal lobe symptoms such as short-term memory loss, difficulty with decision making, inability to recall names or details and confused thinking. People with traumatic stress disorders, depression, anxiety disorders, alcohol or chemical dependency may have memory and thinking difficulties that imitate Alzheimer's disease. Dehydration can result in bladder and lung infections and confused thinking. Some medicines depress memory such as antihistamines (in some allergy or sleep medicines) or anticholinergics (in some pain or incontinence medicines).

Prevention programs and early treatment of these conditions can restore most or all of healthy brain function and avoid further degeneration. Decline of brain function leads to more reliance on a caregiver who is probably already overwhelmed with the challenges of family life and survival especially in Armenia, a country rich in history and culture, but struggling once again to rise economically and politically. Inexpensive national programs such as adding iodine to salt or folate and niacin to wheat products can bring important minerals and vitamins to the general Armenian population and thus prevent thyroid-related or vitamin B-related dementias. City dwellers may enhance nutrition with produce from small gardens such as the Armenians in rural and mountainous regions where vegetable gardens and fruit trees enrich diets with anti-oxidants and foods rich in vitamin B, such as dark green vegetables, legumes, meat, eggs and dairy products (like madzoon). Also important are the consumption of ten to twelve glasses of water (or other liquid) a day, avoiding anti-memory drugs, avoiding alcohol or tobacco; hormone balance, and treating infections, heart and circulation problems, stress, depression, or related disorders.

Vascular Dementias

Many people have long-standing heart or circulation conditions that impact blood flow to brain cells (neurons). Some people suffer from diabetes – especially poorly controlled diabetes, high (or too low) blood pressure or high levels of cholesterol/triglycerides, and heart conditions such as rhythms that may be uneven, too fast or too slow that thus send an uneven flow of blood or clumps of blood cells to the brain. Diagnosing and treating the underlying condition may slow the damage to neurons, prevent a major stroke and extend the person's ability to remain self-sufficient. Sometimes a pacemaker is necessary to regulate or strengthen the heartbeat. Aspirin and similar medicines, a good diet, exercise, and reduced stress help. Any quick changes, such as sudden memory loss, slurred speech, or weakness in any part of the body, are signs of stroke, an emergency, and treatment such as aspirin or related medicine within three hours can minimize brain damage.

Alzheimer's Disease

Alzheimer's disease, the most commonly occurring progressive dementia, affects more than four million Americans and worldwide from five to twenty percent of those over sixty-five years of ages. The dementia is slow and progressive. Alzheimer's disease is not normal to aging, not contagious, and not caused by aluminum pots or pans.

Alzheimer's disease may be described in three stages. In the first stage, Forgetfulness, there are usually problems with short-term memory and language, especially recalling the names of people or objects. At this stage the person is nearly self-sufficient in activities at home; reminders such as a note, a calendar, a timer that buzzes, a phone call or a friendly word from a family help. In the second stage, Confusion, there is progressive memory loss, decline of ability to perform routine tasks at home or work, clumsiness with mechanical tasks or skilled movements such as eating or grooming, confusion about the time (date or year) and location (not knowing the correct street or city), and decreased comprehension. Over time other difficulties may arise such as struggles with decisions, not finishing tasks, and decline in personal care; a caregiver should be readily available to provide occasional assistance. In the third stage, Severe Dementia, the person needs constant assistance and supervision. The person who used to bathe regularly, change clothes appropriately and dine with the family now may try to wear the same clothes every day, wear too many or not enough clothes, refuse to bathe or shower, avoid time with the family, and later be unable to walk, bathe or eat.

Although no cure for Alzheimer's disease exists, now several medicines can shore up the normal memory chemicals of the brain and strengthen brain cells that control memory and thinking skills. A physician may recommend such "memory boosters", or other medication like hormone therapy, vitamin E, B vitamins, anti-oxidants and, in the future perhaps, some experimental drugs such as a vaccine or beta secretase lowering substances.

Help

Family education and sharing the care provide major help with adjustments regarding long-term care. Early education of the primary family caregiver, typically a woman, and planning with all the family members will prepare them for unexpected or sudden changes. The primary family caregiver in the Armenian diaspora family should think in terms of the whole family unit including the patient, the extended family, friends, and neighbors. Partnering with health experts, community, and church groups can ease the care and is essential to avoid overwhelming the primary family caregiver. An important factor in avoiding her collapse is training the other male and female members of the family to share the burden of care giving as well as the other daily needs and duties that help the family to function. Young children can read stories or take walks with the grandparent. Neighbors can exchange services. The church network in Armenia has strong spiritual, political and social relationships and should consider providing services such as Day Centers for elders so that family caregivers can attend school, go to work, or have respite—all essential for survival of the family. Support groups can give emotional support and pragmatic, simple suggestions about care.

Because of the slow, long-term decline of progressive dementia, care giving is taxing. The female caregiver who already shoulders major family care responsibilities plus works outside the home may sacrifice her own health, thus leading to chaos in the family. Caregiver fatigue increases the frailty of females whose health is already more vulnerable to conditions such as diseases of the reproductive system (and related urinary tract problems), autoimmune disease, some gastrointestinal conditions, and infections. A partnership of family, friends and community organizations is essential to provide simple services to the family caregiver to help her deal with duties, her own care and health needs, and to prevent collapse from caregiver fatigue. Resources on Alzheimer's disease follow:

1. Alzheimer's Association: Phone (USA): 800.272.3900 http://www.Alz.org

2. AlzOnLine: Phone (USA): 800.260.2466 http://www.AlzOnline.net

3. Alzheimer's Disease Education and Referral Center (ADEAR): Phone (USA): 800.438.4380 http://www.alzheimers.org

Summary

Family care giving issues in Armenia and the Diaspora are similar in that the primary family caregiver is typically the woman. Healthy lifestyles, early diagnosis and intervention, education and planning ahead from long-term care, and forming a caregiver team will enhance the care and preserve the health of the primary family caregiver as well as the whole family unit. Just as an individual has two separate hands which together can suture a wound, build a shelter, or hold another's hand to form a care giving team, Armenia has the people of Armenia (as one hand) and the people of the diaspora (as the other hand) who can work together for a stronger Armenia—for her families today and for the generations to come.

Leilani Doty, Ph. D., specializes in geriatric, behavioral neuropsychology specific to people with progressive dementia and in women's health issues. As co-founder of the University of Florida's Center for Research on Women's Health, she is the Administrator of its Memory Disorder Clinic. She wrote the Guidebook *Helping People with Progressive Memory Disorders*.

Armenian Women: Expectations for the Future

Svetlana Haroutunian Frunze

On the whole, psychological problems of Armenian women may be classified into two main groups, which in turn may be subdivided into other ones. On the one hand are female problems whose origin does not depend on nationality. On the other hand, specific problems typical of Armenian women correlate with mental and national characteristics.

During the Soviet period, the problem of the Armenian woman was mainly that she was submissive to the Armenian man who was the leader. A woman in submission replaced normal, harmonious relations of collaboration. Thus, the mechanical transfer of terms of V.A. Geodanian's conception of male and female dichotomy into the sphere of concrete psychological and social conformities took place, i.e. the biological laws transferred into social life, and, as a result, male chauvinism obtained its "scientific" substantiation.

Such was the obstacle for an Armenian woman to develop as an individual and present herself in different spheres of life. Her life was limited to the kitchen and to care for her children. Within the last ten years under conditions of political and economic crises, the problems of the Armenian woman have not lessened. On the contrary, they have worsened qualitatively as well as quantitatively. New problems were added to the old ones, which made personal conflicts deepen. Not having established the status of equality with the Armenian man, the Armenian woman has to carry the material burden of the family, from which she had earlier been free. On the other hand, many Armenian men have not been able to endure the changes: they have lost their aims in life, causing one more responsibility for women to carry out in a delicate manner. In addition, it is no secret that many heads of families have set out to earn money abroad, leaving their wives alone to manage housekeeping and take care of the children. Thus, women have found themselves in absolutely strange situations where they perform the function of father as well as mother. As a result, the traditional Armenian family has collapsed because of the displacement of social sex roles, causing a chain of changes. Thus, the Armenian woman is in a very difficult situation. Dramatically changed conditions of life did not allow her to adapt quickly enough to reveal herself harmoniously as a wife, mother and, of course, as a member of society on the whole. All these may cause personal conflicts to arise that will, no doubt, affect her family on the whole, and children in particular. This will bring a threat to the stability and health of the family as a cell of society. These facts reveal that the Armenian family cannot survive and develop without State support.

Svetlana Haroutunian Frunze chairs the Psychology Department at Yerevan State University.

How to Raise Public Awareness and Spirituality: The Role of Women in a Democratic State

Margarita Gurdjieff

Today, modern civilization is in a crisis, in a state of changing values and stereotypes. People are worried about global problems such as impending economic and ecological catastrophes, increase in the population of our planet, poverty, disease, unemployment, etc. All of the aforementioned complicate the situation and create social and economic inconsistency. They influence individuals and cause psychic and physical problems. Armenia is a particular case where all these problems are exaggerated.

The protection of health and the preservation of surroundings are in close relationship to one another. Nowadays there is an increase in so-called "diseases of the age" which include cardio-vascular, oncological and allergic diseases and psychological disorders. In addition, diseases such as influenza and other acute respiratory infections and viral diseases are widespread. Evaluating this situation we see that these pathologies restrict adaptability of the human organism. People are trying to find ways to survive these crises and overcome economic problems because any local or regional problem causes lack of balance in the entire world.

Our experience of life teaches us an important truth: the new symbols of marketing in our civilization must be esthetics, morality and justice. For the realization of those purposes, everyone must trust his consciousness. We must have a serious dialogue about spiritual health—spiritual health in harmonious relationship with the physical being. The breaking of this relationship is dangerous. People are ready to overcome old conceptions, stereotypes and the existing "cultural shock." The different experiences and obstacles that Armenians have faced during history allow for the development of strong spiritual potential based on education and concepts of Armenian origin.

Paths to Spiritual Development

There are different paths to spiritual development, which require attention of the public and the government.

I) Education, culture and science must cooperate and develop the role and effectiveness of education. Teachers who have modern conceptions must have the opportunity to improve the educational system. New colleges and institutions must be opened for preparing professional governing staff for Armenia. All students, regardless of their social class, must have equal rights in education. There must also be programs developed to support talented children who do not have sufficient finances to study.

II) With the help of economic policies, including investments, finances from other donations expand cultural, artistic, educational and creative activities in different disciplines.

III) Provide all necessary conditions for women to live without discrimination. Let women have a limitless access to information (an educated woman is an important contribution to civilized society).

Provide access for women in economic and political activities to a level of making decisions.

Develop the highest standards of life so that there is no gender discrimination as in countries like Sweden and

Norway. Women have to overcome discrimination by raising self-awareness and developing their rights and powers in the society. They should also strengthen their role in different areas such as economics, politics, culture, etc.

IV) Create non-political means of mass information and let people learn and study different cultures and values.

V) Activate economic and legal mechanisms to protect science and culture.

VI) Make the self-awareness of every civilian free of old discrimination and stereotypes. These stereotypes must be considered:

Change the general thinking, in which people always rely on their leaders and think that only leaders are responsible for the good of their country and the nation. Everyone must take his/her part in bettering the created situation. The self-awareness of each citizen must take him/her to a level of new responsibility for his/her nation and homeland.

In the former Soviet Union, people were tired of their civic duties. We are at a turning point in history, but our homes are endangered and our families under the threat of obliteration. Everyone must make his/her choice and decisions in life and not let others decide for them.

Armenians have had a tragic history, many times ruled by others, and slaughtered so that an inferiority complex was created. However, there have been many accomplishments which played a great role in the civilization of nations. Armenians must get rid of our inferiority complex. Everyone should first of all respect himself/herself and should acquire national dignity and perform civic duties.

There are ideas espoused to have Armenian culture assimilated in European and American cultures. But this is not a true way of renovating a society. People must get rid of dogmatic thoughts and should acquire a creative and reasonable way of thinking. It is better to create a unity of different cultures which are enriched by one another.

Various countries are concerned about pressing the strong will and national spirit of small nations by threatening them with the fear of global disasters. Armenian citizens shouldn't be afraid. Armenian ancestors have faced such trials in life that generations have acquired genetic immunity. It is time to revive our national Armenian spirit and be able to guide our destiny with our hands.

The bureaucratic way of thinking in life led many Armenians to social indifference to the absence of love and interest in once-creative abilities. We must maintain a very simple idea: authority that should act for the sake of the public, and not the reverse. If the state organizations do not satisfy the basic interests of society, these organizations will be distracted and new ones will be formed to protect society. These results depend on us, men and women civilians and on our activity in social and political life.

We must eliminate totalitarianism. We must finally understand that no one has the right to control the truth. Every civilian must have his/her part in discovering the truth. We may reach agreements by means of dialog and by arguing various concepts, and not through fighting. But these are considered a strong social and political passivity in performing civic duties in Armenia. In most cases, the main cause of social passivity is the patriarchy in families. This creates a situation where it is easy to manipulate general thinking which in turn becomes useless. In a very short while, society should be transformed from its passive state into a creative, developed and mature society.

Talented people and their creative abilities are neither noted nor respected. There is an erroneous social conception, which explains that everyone is equal, and that anyone is allowed to do whatever he/she likes, he/she only needs the proper conditions and positions, resulting in a social leap where people have moderate abilities but higher ambition. People must respect talents. Different powers in society must cooperate and give birth to a new concept, which will allow them to move forward and overcome the neglect and deadlocks that formerly existed.

A rebirth of public self-awareness is possible in two ways:

1) By raising the self-awareness of the people themselves.

2) By inculcating spiritual participation in the people.

Spiritual and material activities must create together one strong power, which will raise the energy of people and let them overcome difficulties. The self-awareness of every Armenian must become free of internal stresses, old conceptions and stereotypes that restrain the creative activities of people in the process of recognizing and forming a democratic population.

Margarita Gurdjieff qualified as a philologist and teacher of Russian Language and Literature from the State University of Samarkand. She has taught in Karpi Village and #256 Kindergarten in Yerevan. She is also president of Karap, Ltd. She qualified as a practical psychologist and was elected a full member of the Russian Natural Sciences Academy.

ORAL TRADITION AND FOLKLORE

Sharyn S. Boornazian, moderator

Stories are an international currency. Much of our informal learning is captured in personal stories. Stories are both a process and a product. Our speakers use oral tradition and folklore to teach and to capture what is learned from the past and carried into the present. Storytelling helps us grow to greater self-knowledge. The skills, knowledge and values of a people and culture are captured in our stories. The absence of story leads to isolation; the richness of story opens our minds to other cultures and ideas. We are human because we tell, and listen to, stories. Written and spoken stories help a culture find and keep a voice. Listeners and participants come to appreciate the life paths of others: the diversity of culture, ethnicity, nationality, language, religion, environment, health, opportunity, political strategies, family, outcomes and expectations.

How often do we use a story to make sure someone understands what is important? The same story heard or told at different life points evokes different questions or interpretations. This telling— the performance, the ritual— reveals what is important and often leads to a greater understanding and appreciation of the people, history and customs. Stories told, stories written, stories heard and reflected upon make a difference in the context and direction of our lives. Frequently personal stories act as a bridge between experience and an academic discussion.

Where do we exchange stories today? Does it happen in a conference like this? Storytelling allows people normally separated by schedules, social class, occupation, and neighborhoods to come together as a community. The church, town square, campfire and front porch are frequent storytelling sites. Perhaps the copy machine and the automobile are the twentieth century campfires, certainly email and the internet are fast becoming a folk medium for the twenty-first century. Regardless of the where and how, oral tradition and folklore provide us with a walk-around memory.

Armenian Rituals and Traditions in the Socialization of Children

Emma Petrosyan

In Armenia, as in other societies, an important aspect of raising children is to socialize them and prepare them for their future rôles as adults by teaching them the traditions of their culture. Thanks to the efforts of teachers, ethnologists, and amateur folk dance groups at various cultural centers for the education of children, Armenian society is now enjoying a revival of these very popular rites and traditions.

Ethnologists separate Armenian traditional rites into "calendar" and "non-calendar" events. Although both children and adults participate in the celebration of these rites, children have separate rôles. Moreover, according to old beliefs, children, particularly very young girls because of their innocence, have a sacred influence on the fertility of nature.

Lullabies are the earliest of these ritual activities. They promote the development of the infant's sense of rhythm and the perception of high-pitched sounds. Singing lullabies is also considered a means of dispelling evil. At the age of 4-5 months a child responds and reacts to surroundings, but growth at this age is slow.

Like other peoples, Armenians associate growth with height. Therefore to promote growth, many rites for a young child include dances that incorporate repeated jumps. These jumps are perceived to evoke the magical process of growth.

One ritual dance, that combines melodic recitation with text, is called *ver-veri* (up, up—higher up). In this tradition, as the baby is being dandled, growth in stature is invoked and the child trained not to fear heights. The text of the recited charm has many variants. It can be long or short in different ethnographic regions of Armenia. Two lines of the text however, are consistent.

| թռի, թռի, թռցնեմ | fly, fly, I'll make you fly |
| սեւ հաւի միս կերցնեմ | I'll feed you the meat of a black hen. |

The black hen is a very popular image in Indo-European mythology. The hen, especially a black hen that lays golden eggs, is connected to the image of the Great Mother as the source of life. The hen's black color is also a metaphor for the black color of earth and is associated with Mother Earth. Moreover, in Armenian, the word *hav* means both bird and ancestor. It is also possible that the line, "I'll feed you the meat of a black hen," also conveys the idea of sacrifice and the eating of that sacrifice as a way of becoming one with the ancestor.

Another traditional rite takes place upon the appearance of a baby's first milk tooth. In this celebration, as a charm is being recited, a mixture of boiled grains of wheat and raisins are sprinkled over the baby's head. Often a woman in the group squashes a grain of the boiled wheat and places it on the baby's first tooth. These acts are believed to guard against the evil eye and to impart the idea of fertility or of abundance: much grain—many teeth.

Soon babies begin to learn children's rhymes and games. They learn to clap their hands and develop a sense of rhythm. A comparison of the variants on clapping games reveals two basic versions. The nonsense words rhyme and have rhythm, but have no special meaning.

| Ծափիկ, ծափիկ, ծիրանի | Clap, clap, purple |
| ծուռը խայմախս կռլմանի | the sea is as smooth as cream |

or

Դռպլլ, դոմպլլ, մադարա Tat-a-tat, rat-a-tat little drum
հարս կ՛բերեմ կխաղա   I'll bring a bride and she'll dance

The first variant with the words *dzirani dzov* (purple sea) is the more interesting one. It is reminiscent of the words "*Dzov dzirani*," in the pre-Christian poem "The Birth of *Vahakn*," recorded by Movses Khorenatsi (Moses of Khoren) in his *History of the Armenians* (1978), where the same metaphor, երկներ ի ծովն ծիրանի (the purple sea was in travail) is used. In any case, the expression invokes birth and childhood.

Another rhythm teaching game, still widely played in Armenia, can also be seen as an invocation of the idea of height and the miracle of growth. Four to six children participate in the game. The players pinch the backs of their hands and their partner's hands with the thumb and index finger, thus creating a column of hands. The column of hands is moved up and down to the accompaniment of a song or recitative.

There are numerous versions of the rhymes recited as the game is played. A comparison of the texts reveals a common last line. Two examples are given here:

Ծիվ, ծիվ, ծիտռնա   Twit, twit, twidona
հարսը տարան Մադռնա   my bride was taken to Madona
ես Մադռնի տղեն ըմ   I am a son of Madona
թագավորի Ջեւեն եմ   I am the king's son-in-law
թռ,...ռ,...պապոնց երդիկը   fly, fly, to your father's home

or

Ծիվ, ծիվ, ագրավա ծիվ   Twit, twit, a crow's twit
ագրավ գ՛նաց Երուսադեմ   the crow went to Jerusalem
բուրդ գվեց, բամբակ բերեց   he carded wool, brought cotton
իմ Shգրանին շապիկ կարեց   he sewed a shirt for my Dicran
թռ,...ռ,...պապոնց երդիկը   fly, fly, to your father's home

In both versions children imitate the twittering and flight of birds. The first lines begin with a nonsense word that sounds like the twittering of birds. In the first version, the bride is compared to a bird. In the second, the image is that of a crow that flies to Jerusalem, brings wool and cotton, and sews a shirt for the child Dicran. "թռն...ն..." in the last lines imitates the beating of wings flying towards the ancestral home. At the end of the game the children flutter and wave their hands, imitating the flight of birds which could be interpreted as a symbol of growing up.

Although parents have a more active rôle in the rites connected with protection from evil, the participation of children imparts a ritual purity to these rites. Consider the feast of Ascension, when fortunes for the coming year are told. On Ascension eve, personal objects are placed in a basin of water together with flowers and herbs. The basin, covered with a veil, is exposed to the stars during that magical night. The next day, a young girl, so innocent that "she does not know from which direction the sun rises," is selected to pick objects from the basin while their owners' fortunes are read from a special book of divination.

As children grow older, they are included in the life of the society at the same time they are being taught the traditional norms of behavior. In the past, children took part in all the calendar and situational feasts. An analysis of the cycle of these traditional feasts reveals that each feast represented a boundary between the past and the future: one thing has ended and another has begun. Each calendar feast represented a New Year, not in the astronomical sense, but in the cycle of agriculture and cattle breeding. The participation of children in these New Year rites was very important. Some of the most popular rites are listed below:

1. The participation of children was especially important on January 5th. According to ancient beliefs, this day was the birthday of the Child-New-Year. Grandfathers would cut the traditional ritual loaf of bread that contained a baked-in coin. The ritual loaf was sliced on the back of the youngest boy in the family, for whom this was a very important and happy occasion.

2. The most popular tradition at Christmas was the house to house procession when children danced and sang songs. A mummer, usually a boy dressed in a goat costume and dancing comically, led the procession. The children sang *Avedises,* or carols, and called the grandmother of the house to come out. They blessed the house and asked for gifts. The women would come with gifts of eggs, butter, flour, and fruit.

3. At the beginning of Lent, grandmothers prepared an *Aklatiz,* or a fetish. The fetish, symbolizing the soul of the demon, was an onion stuck with seven feathers, representing the seven weeks of Lent. The grandmother would hang the fetish from the smoke hole in the ceiling. At the end of each week, one of the children in the family would climb to the ceiling and throw down a feather from the fetish. The diminishing number of feathers in the fetish indicated the approach of Easter. The grandmother would tell the children their fortunes. Children believed that the fetish kept a vigilant watch over them, therefore they were especially dutiful and kind to members of their family during Lent.

4. A tradition using rattles, called *karkacha,* took place on Palm Sunday. On that day children, holding their *karkachas,* would stand at the church door. When the religious ceremony was over, each child would try to strike the shoulder of a worshiper leaving the church with a *karkacha.* In this rite, the child is blessing an adult. The ringing sound of the *karkacha* was believed to protect the person from evil spirits at the same time it imitated the chirping of birds. In the afternoon, the children held processions. As they went from house to house they danced and sang, blessing the family's members and asking for gifts. Housewives gave them eggs and flour.

5. The whole community participated in the celebration of Ascension Day. As described earlier, young girls led the festival and were the center of the ceremony.

6. Drought had very serious consequences for the harvest. In the old days, peasants held a ceremony calling for rain. Grandmothers prepared dolls for the children. The dolls, which were called fiancées of rain, were dressed in costumes that included brooms. Members of the family gave eggs and flour to the children and threw water on the dolls and little girls.

7. In the thirteenth century the church celebrated a rite where ten boys were chosen to play the parts of young women in the enactment of the parable of the "Wise and Unwise Virgins." A platter held ten notes, five of which were marked "wise" and the other five marked "unwise." The boys drew their fortunes; the five unwise were thrown out of the church.

8. At Easter the boys held a competition to see who had the strongest egg. They rolled the eggs down a slope, buried them underground, and tried to find them.

Conclusions:

All the traditions and rites discussed here have a special social meaning. Children were trained to behave with discipline in society. Their bestowal of blessings on adults is a form of respect for their parents and elders. The participation of children in processions showed their respect, tolerance, and subordination to the leaders of their society and the organizers of the rites. The rites also serve a cultural function. Children are taught to dance, sing songs, prepare masks, and play games. The rites gave children social skills and taught them tolerance in their society.

Work Cited:

Moses, of Khoren. 1978. *History of the Armenians*. Translated with commentary by Robert W. Thomson. Cambridge: Harvard

University Press. [This work is also available in classical Armenian and other languages.]

Emma Petrosyan, Ph. D., from Yerevan State University in historical studies, is head of the study group on Folk Theater and Ethnochoreology. She is the Senior Researcher of the Institute of Archeology and Ethnography, National Academy of Sciences. Dr. Petrosyan has organized many folk and dance group and has pub;lished over 100 books and articles in these fields and has received many awards and prizes.

The Revival of the Ancient Art of Storytelling: Empowering the New Generation with Traditional Stories

Alidz Agbabian

When my children were born over 20 years ago, I faced an urgency to weave together the pieces of my diasporan identity. As a parent, I sensed the responsibility I now had to help my children discover their human potential with tools from their own inherited national cultural heritage. And since early on my children had shown an interest in books, one of the first things I did was to put together a library of Armenian children's books.

However, it did not take me long to realize that quality children's books were hard to come by in the Western Armenian dialect—the dialect of our family. Soon I found myself reading stories aloud from collections in the Eastern Armenian dialect published in Armenia and presenting them to my children in the dialect they understood.

It was during these daily storytelling sessions on the living room carpets and cushions, that my children made me realize the power of the spoken word. Despite the fact that they routinely had access to beautifully illustrated American picture books, electronic games, toys and endless television programs, my children were willing to listen to the stories I narrated to them without books or illustrations. And the more stories they asked for, the more I became convinced that they could be nurtured and guided through the God-given living word, transformed by their imagination into imagery and visions. Visions, which like guardian angels, could oversee their small, precarious steps, and lead them towards becoming independent and responsible human beings with a strong sense of cultural identity. Thus, during my search for an Armenian cultural entity which my children could relate to from an early age, I found myself on the shores of the vast ocean of our oral traditions: folk and fairy tales, myths and legends, folk games, folk songs, fables, riddles, dances, blessings, prayers, the epic poem—a heritage shaped by the relationship of this ancient nation with its environment and the cosmos. By word of mouth and by way of the spiritual inner journey of my people, this heritage had arrived at the threshold of the twenty-first century. Today it is offered to us by the sacred work of many devoted collectors.

Beyond the Armenian community, I was also inspired and guided by the American storytelling revival, which had stared in the 1970s and is still gaining strength. This is a revival not only of the ancient tradition of storytelling, bringing together a diversity of ethnic as well as personal and family lore, but also a revival of the persona of the storyteller. Today in the United States, the National Storytelling Network represents over 500 professional storytellers. Through community storytelling evenings, local and international festivals, conferences and publications it brings together thousands of teachers, librarians, amateur groups and individuals. As a participant in the storytelling movement, I witnessed how people in this scientifically and economically most advanced society had the need to reevaluate the most fundamental form of human expression—the spoken word.

It is from this premise that I had a chance to look anew at my own tradition—the Armenian oral tradition. As the stories started unfolding their messages to me, I realized that I was becoming the first beneficiary of the storytelling experience. (That is why I think the three apples in the traditional ending of Armenian folktales is always first for the teller.) Through the telling, I entered into the enchanted garden of my people's spirit. While in my consumer driven society the day could be saturated with endless uninspiring, unrelated, fragmented daily duties, the oral tradition of my ancestors offered the reverse— imagery that integrated my soul and mended the fragmentation of the day. These images, pouring from the humanity of my people, depicted an ageless time, where the smallest of routine daily movements and the grand movements in nature are perceived as one. The rocking of the baby in its cradle, the patterns of a grandmother's lace, the sowing and harvesting of wheat, the rustle of trees, the rising and setting of the sun and moon were perceived equally as part of the bigger eternal movement of Creation, of the mystery of the universe. Thus they were all sacred and eternal. Like the energy trapped in an atom, the oral tradition harbored ageless meanings, which when released through the spoken word, could connect me to the eternal in my daily life today.

Children instinctively respond to this connecting power of the spoken word if only early on we give them a chance to relate to the medium and its carrier—the oral tradition. Children, born from the Spirit, recognize the Spirit in themselves. Jesus said "Let the children come to me and do not hinder them, for the Kingdom of God belongs to them." We, as caretakers, often disconnect and interrupt the children from their creative strains of inspiration with our shortsighted educational approaches. Children can teach us. We can learn from them. When I tried to explain, first to myself, then to principals and educators, the importance of the ancient stories of our tiny nation to the twenty-first century, the response of the children in my storytelling groups, and in turn, of their families, became a living testimony for their timelessness. Without any sense of obligation, the children enthusiastically responded to the meaningful premises of the stories, related to their characters and fundamental values. They took the stories home and related the messages to other family members. They came back and asked for more. The stories crossed age boundaries; the child as well as the grandfather discovered different depths of meaning in the same story. It became obvious to me, that away from the homeland it would be possible to create a fertile ground for the education of the diasporan Armenian children through oral traditions—traditions that enable us to look into the kaleidoscope of imagery in the souls of our people, woven by their special talents with the sounds and rhythmic patterns of their unique living language, folk music, and the color, form, space and movement patterns of their folk art; traditions that continuously renew themselves and the messages they bring to the growing children of the next generation, no matter where they live, no matter what the economic and scientific development level of the society they live in.

Today, in our busy lives, we can keep the children entertained for hours with the touch of a button. But by keeping them busy with fast paced electronic games and violent TV programs, which reflect our exceedingly violent urban societies, we put the children into bondage and enslave them with addictive behaviors. The endless marketing of highly exciting entertainment media disconnects the children early on from the awareness of their emotions and creativity. The child has no time to be with himself/herself, to be selective of whatever is being offered to him/her from the outside and to create his/her own imagery from within. In this environment, adverse to human spiritual growth, how can the child be focused, how can he/she try to build his/her individuality, and why would he/she express himself/herself in Armenian—a language that is not the language of the current seductive popular culture?

Learning to read and write Armenian is the next treacherous step, and beyond that very little prepares them to relate to the Armenian literary, musical and artistic traditions. We still have not thought of an antidote to the prevailing popular market-driven culture; we have not given the children the tools to build the foundations for realizing their human potential from their inherited cultural identity. In this regard, in my selection of stories, I pay special attention to the plight of girls. The passage of girls into adolescence and a self-valuing adulthood has become exceedingly tumultuous in today's patriarchal, war-loving, aggressive, relentlessly market-driven competitive societies. How much more our young girls need to relate to the strong but nurturing female archetypes of our tradition!

Like today's computers, our oral tradition is a branch of our culture that is portable. It will travel with us anywhere and everywhere, from childhood to deep maturity, from Armenia to America. Even after the creation of the Armenian alphabet, our people, living and toiling on the land, adhered to their oral tradition with an inner penmanship through patterns of imagery and memory. I would like to call that tradition inner Armenian history, a history of spiritual development. And why in the century of the Internet should we not be able to continue this tradition; something which our nation has done for centuries? Do we stop talking when we learn reading and writing? Likewise the oral tradition needs to converse with us in order not only to survive, but to extend its full capacity to us. And this is possible. In my experience, I have seen that this conversation is possible. Even after several years and without the fear and pressure of grades and tests, children remember with joy the details of a story that they had listened to of their own free will with pure enjoyment. When later, the child tries to recreate in his/her mother tongue moments of the story he/she has enjoyed and related to, teaching him/her to read and write in Armenian is easy. He/she now has a personal experience that motivates him/her. When parents show gratitude to me for instilling in their children love towards their culture, I remind them that the power is in the culture that it is given to us.

Let us lend an ear to the following Armenian myth:

Once a young bride was kneading dough when her mother-in-law reprimanded her, telling her the dough was stiff. The bride was not supposed to talk back to the elderly, but gently responded by saying "Gagoogh eh, gagoogh eh,"—"It is soft, it is soft." Nevertheless every time the bride kneaded the dough the mother-in-law reprimanded her telling her the dough was stiff. "Gagoogh eh, gagoogh eh," would respond the bride.

And one morning when the bride was kneading the dough the mother-in-law cursed her. As a response against her mother-in-law's harsh words the bride transformed herself into a dove and flew out the window into the vast blues sky. And they say to this day, if you wake up early in the morning and lend an ear to the cooing of the doves, you will hear them sing, "Gagoogh eh, gagoogh eh," which means "It is soft, it's it's soft…"

This myth is not about the disobedience or defiance of the bride. The dough is a symbol of her soul, which she knows is soft, pliable, transformable and nurturing. Recognizing this, the bride is connected to her soul, and she will always be true to her voice.

And our souls are true to the voice of our race, coming to us from the deepest level of our cultural awareness—our oral tradition. Whether or not we have borne children, as nurturing female representatives of our generation we are responsible for building the identity of the next generation. Our ancient oral tradition, shaped through the experiences, the talents and the faith of our people, patterned to fit our genetically inherited temperament today, brings to us endless stories from the cumulative psyche of our nation. From the first lullaby we sing to our newborns, the prayers we whisper into their ears, to the epic of David of Sassoon, this tradition is the foundation of our national

cultural heritage. It is up to us to open up its tremendous powers to the new generation, by giving it the place it deserves in
our families, communities and educational systems.

Storyteller Alidz Agbabian was born in Lebanon and is a graduate of Yerevan State
University. She presents folk and fairy tales, myths, and fables from her Armenian
heritage as well as from the Middle East, Mediterranean basin, and Newly Independent States. She is author-publisher of children's stories, songs, and picture books; the
most recent is *Ayp for Soup*.

Woman as Creative Personality

Arousiag Sahakyan

My observations regarding women's issues are based on interviews conducted among middle aged and older women, both in Armenia and the diaspora (Los Angeles, Aleppo, Toronto). I have considered active women—scientists, artists, professionals, leaders, and members of organizations: women whose educational and creative rights have not been and are not limited. As a reference for comparison, I have also interviewed women in vocational positions as well as housewives. Furthermore, I have offered the same interview to men in high-ranking positions. For me, the following observations are most important:

a. Both in Armenia and the diaspora the answers to the questions are identical—an equal gender national character which is a mark of solid and traditional identity.

b. In regard to the identical nature of the answers, economic status does not play a role: the answers of a Los-Angeles-based intellectual living a comfortable lifestyle and that of a financially less fortunate intellectual of the homeland are similar.

First Viewpoint: Internalized Compliance (Acceptance)

Women demand rights and equality equivalent to men. Women perceive their freedom and rights only in comparison to men. Men do not accept this comparison. Why do women take men as their criterion for rights and freedom? Are men truly or absolutely free? Do they have absolute or real rights? Women do not consider this issue and this is their biggest shortcoming. When women's rights are not investigated as part of a national reality – as a reality of a given time in the national history – the process becomes self-limiting and unfruitful.

Today's men in Armenia are jobless. In the context of our national perception, men as the primary providers have fallen outside the boundaries of any kind of rights and freedom. The man standing beside the woman is in a weakened position. Hence, is it logical today to be demanding equality with men? We have stereotypical visions: a patriarchal vision of our families where the wife can not even open her mouth and is bound to be at home while the man has all the freedom outside.

Realities were very different in the nineteenth century as well. In order to be able to pay government taxes, men used to leave their village homes and go to foreign cities. All of the heavy burden of labor in the villages—working the land, sowing, irrigating, and harvesting, in addition to taking care of the children and the elderly, fell on women's shoulders. Women took on the role of men. So whenever it was essential, the Armenian women, like the men, came out of the house and became the breadwinners of the family. This is also today's reality. Does it mean that the exiled husband is free, while the wife bound to the home is not? What are the equalities we are seeking in this instance? Equating our freedom to equality with men has the following ramifications:

a. Women have accepted and continue to accept the idea that men are endowed with a special kind of freedom.

b. Such an acceptance is internalized and frustrates both men and women and further obstructs women's claims for their rights.

c. Equality with men as a criterion first and foremost helps men, confirming their real or attributed freedom and rights. Hence, by comparing themselves to men, women are positioning themselves in a losing situation.

Second Viewpoint: Confrontational Awareness

The ideas of freedom and rights have always had and will always have other criteria, independent of gender, nationality, or governmental and societal systems and time. In such concepts as freedom and rights, men are not the norm, and freedom is not men's prerogative. Men have either conquered or are given external freedom. This type of freedom is also offered to them by women. Men establish themselves in this false freedom, take advantage of it, and violate women's rights.

Women with an awareness of their essence and biological nature do not want to accept these superficial norms of freedom, do not want to be subordinate to a superiority which is not authentic. Women do not want to exploit the freedoms which men take advantage of in matters of sexual rights, family responsibilities, and job and management positions. This viewpoint places women in a stronger position, but contains yet another danger; by a confrontational attitude of freedom perceived as relative to men, women are narrowing the field of their rights and activities, and hence once more violating their own rights.

Men are also perceived as the norm in terms of intellectual/ spiritual and unique creative capacities. It appears that men do not adhere to a comparative norm towards women, that men do not have an issue with trying to be equal to women. Women are not competitors for them, and naturally men become angry when they see a competitor in women. Men set the comparative standards of intellectual/creative abilities. Women reject this. But it is by standards set by men that we ask whether and how much women are given intellectual and spiritual potential. This question would not have existed had comparison not been the norm. This norm also dictates the answer, which takes advantage of the situation: "Yes, women are given rights, but never equal to men."

Men offer evidence that for centuries they have been exclusively gifted in the sciences and arts. Women argue against this
and contend that society, family, and governments founded in
male dominance and governed exclusively by men have not put
forth any demands on women's creativity; they have not given
women opportunity and freedom. Today it appears that the
woman has gained freedom, that society has requested it for
her, and that she has proven herself. But nevertheless women's
capabilities today are still being viewed in relation to men.

Today's issues in this regard and their solutions, even in the
educated sectors of society, seem artificially narrow, with stereotypical ideas put forth both by men and women which in
depth of meaning exclude one another. First the man-woman
comparison in this regard is not correct in itself. It embroils the
issue and complicates the avenues of solutions, propelling it
toward an adversarial position and hence confrontation. And
here women who have struggled against constraint apply the
same confrontational approach, taking advantage of the same
types of freedoms which have been unacceptable to them in men
regarding issues of sexuality, ethics, family responsibilities, jobs,
and governance. The struggle is against different gender in-
equalities, but in fact the gender issue is still the basis of the
matter. Men and women become adversaries who exclude each
other, confrontational yet not reconciled, soliciting their rights
but devoid of freedom.

Folklore and ethnography negate the viewpoint that men,
society, and family have failed to elicit creative activity from
women, and that women have not been given the freedom and
opportunity to be creative. Our oral heritage is proof that women
in all the complex genres such as legend, epic poem, fairy tale,
hayrens, love songs, and dance, have had powerful creative
impetus and great participation. In certain genres women have
been not only the creators but the keepers and the conveyers of
the tradition, as in lullabies and children's games, fortune-tell-

ing, and mourning, as well as in forms of expression like curses, blessings, swearing (oath), and prayer. In all traditional ceremonial rituals women played a role reminiscent of the high position of pagan ceremonial priests.

To be on such a high level of creativity demands freedom, and women had that freedom. Does patriarchy mean concern about norms of everyday living alone? If oral tradition is culture, culture would integrate human relationships in everyday lifestyles and in people's ethics. Wisdom in everyday living stems from respect toward knowledge and tradition. Otherwise it would be impossible to explain how for centuries the Armenian nation, without an independent government and ruled by nations on a much lower developmental level than themselves, has kept in its womb the seeds of continual cultural development and growth and has delivered this mighty cultural inheritance to us.

Enlightening in this regard is the centuries-old truth which is the foundation of the oral and folk traditions. Men and women are two forces disparate and similar, remote and close, opposing and harmonious. Each one is a complete entity. The union of these two entities is absolute perfection. Everything — the four elements of the universe (earth, air, fire, and water), the heavenly light-giving bodies, space and time, the year, the seasons, the months, the days – is equally divided into male and female. The period between the summer and the winter solstice, that is from June 21 to December 21, is considered female dominance. From winter solstice to summer solstice is considered male dominance – six months each. Here is the key to the Armenian legend of Haig. The months of the year are named after Haig's twelve children – six daughters and six sons. Twice throughout the passing year the rules of equality, harmony, and balance are delivered by the two major heavenly light-giving bodies – the sun and the moon – male and female inceptions.

During the spring and fall equinoxes the releasing male energies and receiving female energies of day and night, light and darkness, heat and cold are equal. On March 21, when this equilibrium is followed by the release of the mighty power of the male-sun towards female-earth, the virgin soil is fertilized by the sun and maternally brings forth a new season of the universe and the blossoming of the planet. This is what was celebrated at the beginning of the year, glorifying the absolute harmony of the releasing and receiving active energies. The released male energy does not represent exceptional and unique givens. Receiving female passive energy does not mean second rate and less valuable. In this scheme of equity women were perceived as the symbol of creators-originators, as well as self creators-originators. Mother goddess Anahid is a virgin. Virgin-mother Dzovinar conceived her twin sons from water; God the Father chose the woman, Mary, in whose body He placed His Spirit. This knowledge is much older than any religion.

In the heavens the sun is the male head; and below in the earth-soil is the female foot. Christianity interpreted this as the male being the head and the woman the foot. But is it possible to perceive this as the man being the sole ruler and woman as the submissive, mute complier? The fact that in Armenian tradition the newly wed bride is mute is not a limiting prohibition. That tradition is deeply meaningful. The mystery of the silence of the universe is locked into memory – the memory of the cosmic ocean, of water and earth; and water and earth are female entities. The woman is positioned to be the keeper of memory, and this is the reason why she is traditional and not at all because the sphere of her contacts is limited by virtue of her being locked in the house. To date we use the saying, "The earth will carry the news," "Do good and cast it into the water and it will come back to you." Water and earth have memory. Woman is a grand mistress in charge of transmitting memory; she is a keeper-protectress. This is the key to the Biblical story of creation. Eve and only Eve was granted the mission to pluck the fruit from the tree of knowledge, eating one half and giving the other half to Adam. How is it possible to distort this truth to the point where Eve and her daughters have been charged with the sin of irreversible evil? If Eve's sin is the birthing and creation of mankind and its generations, then what are the blessings bestowed upon her by God?

To my question, "What is a woman?" Armenian women answer, "She is a mother." "But who are you before being a mother and after being a mother?" Just as I have posed this question, I am convinced that the Armenian male also will. I am convinced that if in the soul of the Armenian woman sits a measure of the powerful mother goddess, then within the Armenian male is a man whose perception of the fecundity of nature is tied with this image of the goddess, the goodness of life, and the mystery of human wisdom. Any of today's women's organizations should include an equal number of men. There are no such things as uniquely women's issues. Any concern regarding women is always linked to national issues. Each nation resolves the issues of its male-female relationships according to its national thinking, its centuries-old experiences, and ethnogenesis.

Sublime thought places sublime ideas in the highest circuits of cosmic measures. Below on earth the same measures should be undertaken. That is the commandment "on earth as it is in heaven." Planet Earth is a cosmic body revolving in the universe and subject to its pulsating mystery. If these higher models are not reflected here on earth, then the most sublime idea would turn into the lowliest; and the desired outcome—love and harmony, which represent the first and last design of both women and men—would continue to be a rare outcome.

Arousiag Sahakyan, Ph. D., is senior staff member at the Institute of Archeology and Ethnography of the National Academy of Sciences, Republic of Armenia. A folklorist at Yerevan's Komitas State Conservatory, she is a specialist in national song, rituals, and holidays and the Armenian woman's role in ancient and modern times.

Educating the Youth

Marie Lou Papazian, moderator

The Problems of Schools Providing General Education at the Present Stage

Silva Khrimyan

I want to welcome you and thank those organizing this conference with providing us the opportunity to get together. Your presence here indicates the interest and concern you have for the problems of schools providing general education. The fact that our diasporan colleagues are also taking part in the conference makes us feel extremely grateful; they have always been by our sides and have supported us in providing solutions to the problems we face.

Armenia is a country, where culture and education have always been national values by tradition. The development of education system in Armenia is divided into three stages:

1. Before 1920

The schools were under the protection of the Armenian Christian Church. But in the years of the Independent Republic of Armenia, 1918-1920, the foundations of the contemporary national school were laid.

2. Between 1920 and 1991

In 1920, the Soviet form of government was established in Armenia and the system of Christian schools was changed in accordance with the principles of Socialism.

3. From 1991 to 2000

In the Soviet era, the education system in Armenia was famous for its high standards of educational qualifications and well-developed academic level. But economic and financial difficulties after Armenia declared her independence had an enormous impact on the educational system. Unfortunately, in the early years of that period the problems of the educational system were pushed to the background.

Let us start with a brief description of the current situation in the education system. First, we have the almost complete absence of state investments in the system with all the consequences of low funding: inefficiency of the educational institutions' activity, poor conditions of school premises, lack of teaching staff (underpaid, some teachers leave the school and become involved in other activities), and low participation of parents in solving the current problems in the schools. The end of the Soviet era necessitated reforms in the education system.

In 1997, with the financial support of the World Bank, the educational system started the implementation of a program to improve the system of general education. The program included a transition to a new system of management, the establishment of a textbook renting system, and financial support via grants. The latter provide opportunities to implement various educational programs, investment in new technologies, development of aesthetic, sporting and working education, teachers' training, implementation of new teaching methods, and additional reforms. The new system of management with the establishment of effective school boards aims at solving problems in schools.

In recent years, education programs implemented by various international organizations working in Armenia have strengthened school-community collaboration. The Open Society Institute Foundation, UNICEF-Armenia and Catholic Relief Services have implemented such programs.

Taking into account the importance of information technology in the education system, computer classrooms have been established with computer courses for pupils and teachers thanks to the assistance of a number of international organizations (IREX, OSI Foundation, US Embassy in Armenia) and benefactors.

In different periods schools have received great support from our compatriots and different organizations in the diaspora to overcome the challenges facing them. Organizations as "Knights of Vartan," "Aznavour for Armenia," "Yerevan Cambridge Sister Cities Association" are especially worthy of note. The first two organizations have provided great assistance in building new schools.

The Social Investment Fund of Armenia is also greatly involved in the process of school building. The indispensable condition for promoting the implementation of building operations includes the participation of communities in the financial support (approximately 10 percent of the sum assigned for school building). The schools usually are faced with difficulties while settling this matter as the communities themselves are in need of money and are not able to pay. The problem is often alleviated with the help of benefactors.

During recent years the government of the Republic of Armenia has also allocated a certain amount of money to carry out capital repairs in schools. But these allocations are too small to bring about major improvement in the condition of schools, because of inattention to this work over the years.

Educators are working to improve the curriculum. At the same time investments are going toward new teaching technologies and training of qualified personnel.

I have tried to draw attention to the challenges. I would also like to note that we need more discussions and meetings like this, for they fill us with confidence that there are responsible people who are concerned about the further development of the educational system. I am convinced that this conference, with its scientific and practical orientation, will bridge our efforts and our strengths.

Silva Khrimyan heads the Department of Education of the City of Yerevan.

New Technologies and Communication for a New Millennium

Anna Karakhanyan

Using computers in secondary school is a very important topic for consideration. Our experience proved that this problem is worth of more attention. Why are computers needed in schools? We surveyed different officials, teachers, and principals and received the following answers:

1) to promote students' intellectual abilities;
2) to improve students' thinking in a modern way;
3) to help students develop as full members of contemporary society;
4) to enrich students' ability to apply information learned through Internet access;
5) to prepare students for possible future professional life.

From the information we received, we may conclude that technical perfection is not the most important object. Computer education gives students the possibility to progress, and keeps them abreast of world news. Interactions with their peers help students learn about life in different countries and eventually expand their knowledge with specific examples (text, pictures, videotapes, audio and others). The presence of computers in schools is only ten percent of the matter. Sometimes this computer is just a piece of furniture, sometimes it is not used to its full potential, and other times it becomes out-dated and use-less. In Armenian schools, we give so-called "informatika" lessons, but let us see what we have during and after these lessons:

1) Nearly all these lessons take place without any computer, a senseless action;

2) The President of the Shirak Internet Users Society, George Melkonian mentioned in his recent paper "The Problems of Informatika Teaching" ("Kuimari" newspaper) that teachers gave students only the basics of programming. They teach what they know, for example "Basic" programming language. This method is not effective. Students cannot work on modern computers and cannot put into practice the obtained knowledge. So, it would be better to teach students, using computer programs and searching on the Internet in order to satisfy their inquiries.

3) There are very few computers in each school, limiting student use. Often a computer is located in the principal's office, sometimes for security purposes. Also, only a limited number of students and teachers have sufficient computer experience and knowledge. Thus, the education process has failed. Certainly, every day the conditions get better and now we have computer labs in some schools, thanks to the different programs.

Secondary school #8, named after A.S. Pushkin, previously housed the "Information and Computer Networks Specialists" Association. The Association took an active part in strengthening the relations with the school administration in the computer sphere. Their web site has many interesting facts (http://freenet.am/~pushkin/). The Association soon will organize the second competition of Young Computer Lovers in the school. It is important to note that sixty to seventy percent of participating students obtained their knowledge not in school, but at home or at their parents' offices, simultaneously using computer literature or attending computer courses. So very few students learn computers at their schools. Only the schools which have computer labs and good teachers can give computer knowledge, for example "Anania Shirakatsi" Seminary, "Quant" College and some others. This improved situation is due to different international programs.

Recent Armenian history reveals that, in Soviet Armenia schools, we had not developed and widely spread computer skills. For example, Internet which is now an ordinary tool for each of us, in Soviet times was used only by scientists. Modems became used in Armenia only in 1988 during and after the destructive earthquake. After thirteen years we can see how developed the Internet is in Armenia. Most citizens are familiar with email. We had computers in schools before 1988, but at that time schools did not use them properly. Untrained teachers remain an unsolved problem. Computer experts do not come to our schools because of the low salaries, and only enthusiasts who love their job and love children remain in our schools carrying out their difficult duties.

Nowadays the situation is significantly improved. In Armenia we have several programs whose main goals are to teach children proper use of all computer possibilities, not only as a typewriter or a plaything. I believe that the computer soon will become the main tool for every student and teacher to help them solve many problems of life and study.

Some thoughts about the different computer program activities.

As the main coordinator of the "Three Pomegranates Network" project in Armenia, I can say that in the last three years we have much success. Our Internet site (http://www.3noor.org) will acquaint users with our programs and activities. The computer is a main tool of our program, which networks Armenian and diasporan students through combining efforts in producing creative works. Armenian children living in different countries and establishing personal contacts feel part of an expansive community named Armenian people, with many common traits. We have used in our project new information and computer technologies. In 1997 we organized for the first time in Armenia a videoconference in which children from Yerevan, Los Angeles and Marseilles schools took part. This great event took place on May 9, the day of Shushi Liberation. In spite of time differences and long distances, children not only talked with each other but managed to carry out some creative works and drawings etc.

Our organization is grateful to other education programs. For example the Accels program gave us comprehensive assistance. Some of our program studies have occurred in the schools whose computer labs were organized by Accels. Our program has good connections with the Cambridge Yerevan Sister City Association (CYSCA), with whom we worked from the very beginning. In our program framework, we try to create a small teachers' laboratory with the purpose of assuring the teachers future work in their schools, using prior knowledge and experience.

Some critical questions are:

1) What can Internet give uniquely to young people here?
2) Can young and old people and disabled persons use Internet?
3) How can we better organize computer access?

Special places are needed where those who wish to use the computer have access to Internet. "Internet Café," National library, and the UN office have Internet access. It would be desirable to have more opportunities for free access to Internet. This access is not resolved today because so-called "Public Access" needs huge investments and is very difficult to organize. Establishing computer networks is only a part of the problem. There must be specialists to organize works and teachers to help computer novices. Also, it is very important to assist disabled persons, to provide them with PCs and Internet access. That will allow handicapped persons to improve their living standards. Researchers are investigating this issue and have found some acceptable solutions. Unfortunately, this work has progressed slowly because of insufficient funding. Our disabled citizens have too low an income, so we have to give them free opportunities to exchange information and to make money using their intellectual abilities. More important is to involve disabled children in this process and organize computer labs in the schools where they learn.

In Armenia, another interesting and almost unexamined question is: Can prisoners use a computer? In some countries abroad this question has already been resolved: It needs careful consideration.

Computers and new information technologies have become integrated in the everyday life of Armenians, not only in Yerevan, but also in other cities of the Republic, and let us hope in Armenian villages too. New information technologies are important, not for the isolation of Armenian people, but for the unification of them. The "Three Pomegranates Network" project (previously the "Narod Network" project), which helps Armenian students living in different cities all over the world to better know each other and helps Armenian teachers to use up-to-date education methodology, is an excellent example of positive, progressive use of computers.

It is important that different programs co-ordinate their works and Internet providers assist with new and interesting initiatives. Only in this way will Armenia find her own place in the developing world.

Anna Karakhanyan is the Armenian Main Coordinator of the Narod Network-Narod Institute Mass Media Contact Manager-ARMINCO. She is a graduate of Yerevan State University and is an expert in management information systems, process automation and control, telecommunication services, new information technologies, and computer network design and use.

BUSINESS

Rima Bekirskaya, moderator

Women and Entrepreneurship

It is obvious that in present-day Armenia women are on the periphery of political, social and economic life. They are deprived of the opportunity to influence the decision-making processes. Consequently, the experience of women accumulated in the course of centuries is not utilized while solving national problems.

In April 1998, as a result of the joint initiative of the United Nations office and non-governmental organizations of the Republic of Armenia, the government issued the fundamental tenets of "The program on the improvement of the situation of women." Two months later, "The National Program of activities in 1998-2000 aimed at improving the women's situation in the Republic of Armenia and enhancing their role in society" was approved, too.

The fundamental tenets issued by the government certify, that in the process of building a democratic, legal and social state, the main goal of state policy aimed at improving the situation of women is to ensure their full and equal participation in all spheres of life.

The program clearly states, "About the provision of women's rights in market economy conditions: Working out suggestions and including them in the program of assisting small entrepreneurial activity has the aim of promoting women entrepreneurs who run private business."

Unfortunately, it's not like that.

Today, women's entrepreneurship in Armenia is poorly developed. One of the reasons is the low development level of small and medium entrepreneurship in the transition period from planned economy to free market relations. These are the obstacles:

- Most entrepreneurs are not trained well enough to undertake efficient activity under conditions of market economy.
- Most enterprises are in need of highly qualified specialists in the spheres of accounting, management and marketing.
- Legislation in Armenia is complicated and strict.
- Bureaucracy and corruption.
- Long drawn-out proceedings concerned with customs formalities.
- Institutions contributing to the development of women's entrepreneurship in Armenia are not well developed yet.

On October 1999, the government, on behalf of the Ministry of Industry and Commerce and a number of women's NGOs together with the Konrad Adenauer Foundation, held a seminar on "Women's Entrepreneurship." But it is too early to say that the matter is being settled in Armenia today.

The biggest mistake has been that our leaders and "teachers" tried to borrow the experience of developed countries without taking into consideration our national traditions and existing conditions:

- All these years Armenian women have devoted themselves to assisting their husbands (at the same time trying to remain calm) as the latter were helpless and embarrassed.
- How could entrepreneurship succeed in Armenia in those years: with a rigid blockade and energy crisis, with the population and its purchasing capacity decreasing sharply, with entrepreneurs "paying" local and foreign keepers of the rules for "protection."

- Credit mechanisms practically did not exist. There was only the understanding, "money with percentage," which resulted in the bankruptcy of individual entrepreneurs.
- The complicated and strict administrative laws and taxation system do not contribute to the development of small business.

All these circumstances frightened and pushed away women who wanted to be involved in entrepreneurship. The well-known American formula—a market economy will make people work more efficiently; the better they work the more they will earn—has not worked here.

Problems of Small Business in Armenia

Svetlana Mikhaylovna Minasyan

In Armenia the expression "unemployment has female features" has been transferred presently into "female and entrepreneurship." It is necessary to understand this expression from the point of view of statistical data: Among the 174.4 thousand unemployed people in Armenia, women constitute 124.7 thousand, about 72.5 percent, most between the ages of 30-50. This data is from the Ministry of Social Welfare.

The number of emigrants from Armenia exceeds 20 percent of the population (700 thousand emigrants compared to a 3.5 million population), one-third of which were men who left their families in search of employment abroad.

Using these facts we can draw a conclusion that in the transitional period, accompanied by a sharp decline in living standards, there are women who take the responsibility for taking care of not only themselves but also their children. They became unemployed: 52 percent of these women have higher education, 31 percent have completed secondary education and 17 percent have an incomplete secondary education. Here is another statistical figure: Among the 100 women questioned, 15 percent have an employed husband, 33 percent have an unemployed husband, 31 percent have a husband outside of Armenia and 21 percent don't have a husband at all. With these serious conditions, women start companies of their own, borrow money with a high interest rate or are engaged in unauthorized business and, as a rule, go bankrupt (according to the information from legal procedures for 1995-1998 on companies, banks and private persons declared bankrupt).

Based upon four years of work by the Women's Republican Council of Armenia (WRCA), the development of small and private entrepreneurship in Armenia is proceeding very slowly, especially in rural areas. Specific situations and real conditions are not taken into account although they should stipulate the success factors in work for both public organizations and governmental structures. For business development, the external political, economic, social, legal components are necessary for control and supervision of an internal-method of management.

Entrepreneurship encompasses a variety of economic activity. Entrepreneurship is connected with the management of an enterprise, and that enterprise is comprised of the joint efforts to procure benefits. The necessary qualities that women entrepreneurs must possess are initiative, energy, flexibility, ability to take risks, sharp wits, invention and practicality. In fact, it is impossible to teach a person all these qualities, and it is clear that not everyone is able to become a real entrepreneur. Nevertheless, we believe women can improve their situation with the establishment of their own business during the transition to the market economy. This is why we organized business training for women. Thus, they had the opportunity to run their first business.

In 1995, with support from the Peace Corps, the first business training was organized to explore the social and psychological character of women's adaptation to the new economic policy. We came to the conclusion that, in the future, training should have a specially developed methodology according to the women's proposals. The selection of materials should be carried out and there should be the possibility to attend regular consultations after the trainings. There wasn't one woman entrepreneur to be found in the groups at the seminar on the small and middle-sized business, although a number of people wished to participate in the developing business seminars. In addition, the conditions for small and private business development were more favorable, as many of them had initial capital of their own.

The second period of small and private business development among women in the region was carried out during 1996-1999. In this period our organization tried to find out the reasons for the absence of women entrepreneurs in the region and it turned out that women:

- lose self-confidence;
- begin to feel depression and uncertainty in the future;
- have family stress;
- feel lonely and unwilling to take up new responsibilities;
- lack experience and knowledge in running a business;
- have financial concerns;
- face red tape in the enterprise's registration.

These factors influenced small and private enterprise development among women of the northern region. The problems mentioned above had an adverse effect on the success of their own business. These problems were found out at the time of the trainings and consultations, namely:

- In the transitional period, there is a vast divergence between the efforts and resources used for social development purposes and the achieved results. Policies and organizational structures inherited from the past appear ineffective in present conditions. It indicates that serious reforms in social and economic spheres are necessary. Otherwise our country risks losing its comparative advantages concerning the development and welfare of women and children. Unfortunately, the situation after 1998 does not inspire optimism.

- The main reason for the decline at the development level lies in a decrease in the total volume of production in the region. An ineffective, non-market system of production contributed to a depreciation of domestic products in the world market and the lowering of their rating.

The main goal of the organization was the involvement of women in the private sector and business. In order to implement the task we decided to:

- develop motivation for training and carry out business trainings;
- solve the problem of training;
- organize marketing information for women entrepreneurs;
- hold meetings or found clubs for women entrepreneurs;
- familiarize women with relavant legislation and provide information about it;
- undertake research and analysis in the sphere of business development in the region;
- coordinate business and infrastructure development in the region that is absolutely absent;
- develop credit advantage programs;
- ensure confidence of the population in entrepreneurship and business.

In order to involve women in small and private business within the region, we developed a training program carried out in the cooperation with "The Center of Business Promotion" and "Apricot Plus" under support of the Eurasia Foundation. Two hundred fifty-six women took part in business training; 149 women registered as entrepreneurs in the northern region. Training was given in Spitak, Tashir, Stepanavan, Alaverdi, Dilidjan, and Vanadzor.

Analysis of the trainings showed that the field of small and private business' activities is limited notably by trade, agriculture, handicraft (knitting, fine needlework, macramé, ceramics), food industry, services, seasonal products. There were only 149 women from the whole northern region engaged in business and who have their own businesses. The following information was introduced into the database: the number of employees in an enterprise, the average wages, the volume of raw materials entrepreneurs buy, commodity circulation, and average income (very low showings). Business plans for allocation of credits were also submitted for consideration and discussed there. Business plans were classified according to different spheres and credit programs became an essential component of traning and consultation.

Information gathered from speeches, discussions and participation in various local, Transcaucasian and Russian conferences, workshops on women's situation in the country and improvement of social and economic standards of their living showed common problems in spite of geographical position. As a result, we developed these solutions in the sphere of business and entrepreneurship's development:

- creation of information databases in business;
- establishment of exchange of information system and coordination of business development;
- training of skilled personnel in the business sphere;
- popularization of business and entrepreneurship especially in the sphere of capital markets;
- exchange of working experience and products among women entrepreneurs;
- improvement of the legislation in the sphere of business development;
- working out advantageous credit programs for women.

These recommendations will increase the positive impact of business training.

1. Programs should be long-term.
2. Investors, desirably, worked more with the association and less with the state. The situation of the society isn't

improved from this, but on the contrary it becomes worse.

3. Foundation of the special family bank or a bank for the development of women's business makes the women's place steadier in the state and helps to participate in the acceptance of economic solutions.

4. During the last years many international organizations work less with public organizations, at a time when the NGO itself solves social and economic problems, and promotes the interests of the society.

As one starts her/his conversation about business with Armenian entrepreneurs, they begin to discuss economic problems and express their distrust of the State, Armenia. There are always a lot of reasons, therefore, that it is not worth being engaged in the undertaking, but this is not a way out of the people's difficult situation. They should work because they need money to live and to bring up their children, to strengthen their families and their state. They should not forget that the settlement of social problems comes out of economic issues. Everybody ought to remember the great poverty in our country.

A businessman is not the only one who can make money, but also someone who can relevantly and correctly distribute the money in favor of the society.

We appeal to all the businessmen who want to assist women and Armenian families to regain their genuine entity and be on their way to greater social and economic development.

We'll be grateful for your outstretched hand and will raise it on a pedestal.

Svetlana Mikhaylovna Minasyan is the founder and president of the Women's Association of Armenia, a non-governmental organization with branches in many regions of Armenia. She has multiple scientific publications on the topics of women and business.

Survey on Women's Social-Economic Issues in Armenia

Ofelia Petrosyan

As a result of the country's social-economic reforms, changes have occurred within the economic system. Many enterprises have been closed, which led to the aggravation of social problems, causing unemployment, particularly among women. Women who are breadwinners of the family encountered an especially difficult situation. The number of such families in Armenia reached 55,000 by the start of 1999, and the children cared for in those families number 75,000.

At the transition stage of market relations a small part of the population followed the correct orientation, and through the use of knowledge and opportunities began entrepreneurial activities within a certain economic sphere. With the new political and social-economic situation, men and women faced unequal conditions and are now compelled to operate among businessmen who have reallocated the main resources and property on their own behalf. In light of such competition, women's rights while implementing entrepreneurial initiatives are violated as related to the acquisition or rent of production areas, gaining grants, credits, etc. The need for support for women's entrepreneurial activities is evident, aiming to improve the country's tense social-economic situation.

For this purpose it is necessary to establish a Trans-Armenian Fund Supporting Women's Entrepreneurial Activities that should be directed to:

- support women to start their own business by giving credit with low interest rates,
- create a training and retraining center for women entrepreneurs,
- contribute to the establishment of business relations between the Republic of Armenia and foreign counterparts,
- periodically publish information through mass media, specifically on the Armenian businesswomen's activities and international experience.

The implementation of such measures will enable women to provide self-employment in the economic sphere and provide jobs for women in especially challenging economic conditions, particularly for the solo breadwinners of the family, thus promoting the solution of basic social problems and the foundation for economic development.

Ofelia Petrosyan heads the Women and Children Issues Department of the Ministry of Social Security of the Republic of Armenia.

Personal Journey through Art

Joan Agajanian Quinn, moderator

Another Tongue: Some Notes on Language

Nancy Kricorian

How do you go back to a language you never had? Why should a writer who loves her first language find it necessary and essential to complicate her life with another?—Louise Erdrich

My paternal grandmother, Mariam Kodjababian Kricorian, died on June 19, 1985. In September of 1985 I signed up for my first Armenian language class. Five mornings a week I dutifully trotted up the stairs to a classroom in Kent Hall at Columbia University where the Scottish professor taught a handful of undergraduates and graduates—all of us women—the language of our parents or grandparents.

When I was a child living in the same house with my grandmother, I adamantly refused to learn Armenian. Grandma begged, pleaded, and attempted to bribe me. I didn't want to go to Armenian school in the afternoons or on Saturdays. Growing up in Watertown, I didn't want to know the language spoken by the kids lately arrived from Aleppo and Beirut. At school the other kids—the Italians and the Irish mostly—taunted the immigrants, calling them D.P.'s (displaced persons), F.O.B.'s (Fresh off the Boat), camel drivers and Armo rugbeaters. One girl—a hulking bully—found particular sport in beating up the Armenian girls in the parking lot after school.

In our house, Armenian was the language my father and grandmother spoke when they didn't want us to understand what they were saying. My mother, a non-Armenian who had no interest in learning the language, would narrow her eyes when they spoke to each other, as though she suspected they were plotting against her. Out of loyalty to my French-Canadian mother, I studied French starting in the seventh grade.

But small shards of Armenian imbedded themselves in me despite my resolve. My grandmother told me *"Tooreh kotzeh,"* and I shut the door. She called my uncle *"tootum kloukh,"* and I knew it was an insult. When I misbehaved my grandmother chopped at the air with her hand, threatening *"Kezi geh dzedzem."* *"Amot kezi"* was a constant refrain, inspired by infractions ranging from an untruth to a display of limbs.

After three semesters of Armenian at Columbia, I did a year of night school at the Armenian Diocese. A little while later I tried a class at the Prelacy. In the end I had three textbooks, two dictionaries, piles of note cards, and several notebooks filled with verb conjugations, and I still couldn't speak the language. Admittedly, I had studied French for twelve years and lived in France for over a year before I believed I was able to speak French. Even then the idea that a less than perfect sentence should pass my lips was a horror to me and only after a glass or two of wine would I have called my French fluent.

After my first daughter was born, I gave up studying Armenian. By the time my second daughter was two, I went off on a book tour for my first novel, *Zabelle,* which carried me to different cities in the States and Europe where many Armenians came to hear me read. During the question-and-answer period at a bookstore in Providence, an older woman launched into a diatribe in Armenian. Of the few words I could make out, the one she repeated several times was *"Amot."* I wondered what shameful thing I had done, but someone informed me the woman was castigating several other Armenian-American writers for shameful things they had written. But somehow shame was the response that welled up inside me when I was questioned about my credentials as an Armenian.

"Do you speak Armenian? Are you all Armenian? Is your husband Armenian? Have you been to *Hayastan*? Do you actually know how to bake *cheoregs*?"

After one such grilling, at a reading in Amsterdam, my half-Jewish Dutch publisher said to me, "You have to learn Armenian, Nancy. Then they can't question your credibility. I learned Hebrew and now no one can say anything to me."

So, I found myself a tutor. In her home my tutor speaks Armenian to her son and her husband. Most of her phone calls are in Armenian. In the classroom the language had felt stilted and artificial, but in her home the language was a living, breathing creature.

My tutor had a theory that Armenian was deeply buried in my consciousness and that it would rise miraculously from those depths as I called it forth through use. Unfortunately, this was not the case. The smattering of phrases that I can speak easily has increased, but I'm still wading gingerly into the ocean of this language. *Gamatz, gamatz*, as my grandmother would say.

The Armenian alphabet has two K's, two T's, two P's, two letters for the "ch" sound, and three varieties of R. While I despair of ever being able to spell correctly, I take pleasure in composing short paragraphs with titles such as *"Mer Dooneh"* (Our House) and *"Medz Mayress yev Horyeghpayress"* (My grandmother and My father's brother).

I love that there are different words for father's brother and mother's brother in Armenian, whereas in English we have only "uncle." The Armenian language's precision about family relations, down to having a word for a mother's brother's daughter, demonstrates the strength and potential contentiousness of the Armenian family bond. Learning that the word *"azg"* means nation while *"azgagan"* means relative or kin explained for me my father's attitude that all Armenians are essentially to be treated as cousins.

There is an old Armenian proverb that says, *"Kani lezoo keedess, aynkan mart es,"* which roughly translated says, "As many languages as you know, that's how many people you are." Does that mean that learning a language is a process of becoming a different person?

Of course, all along I've been talking about Western Armenian. This was the language of my grandparents and other diasporan Armenians, which held together a far-flung archipelago of neighborhoods, churches and schools in the communities they reconstituted after the Genocide. For me studying Western Armenian has to do with my grandmother and a time in my life when I lived largely within an Armenian community. I imagine how happy it would have made her to chat with me in the simplest sentences of her native tongue. In fact, acquiring this language is for me a continuing dialogue with her.

Perhaps once the conversation with my dead grandmother achieves an undeniable fluency, I'll take up Eastern Armenian, a language that to this day has its own country.

Years ago when I was in Columbia's Graduate Writing Program, I brought a new poem to class for critique. The instructor, a poet and translator named Edouard Roditi, upon reading the piece remarked, "I assume this is about the Armenian language." I was taken aback. It had never crossed my mind that the poem had a connection with the Armenian language or anything Armenian at all. It was about loneliness.

Saint Pain

You are my mother tongue. Your rules
of grammar are exacting as my breath.
The lungs and that dumb pump fill
and empty, relentless as the clock.

I take your name between my fingers,
and press the letters to my mouth.
Bitter bread I swallow and I love.
The whole alphabet sprouts in my belly,

words grow and twist there, roots
spreading through freshets of blood.
It's a net you cast for me, and I
am lost in your hair. This is

the life I was born for. Milk of pain
made me fat. The waters of my bath
stung like brine. It was this or the blank

rails of my crib. As my cries rose
like prayers, your great hand stretched
down to me. In your fist I felt
the walls of my first home.

Looking at it from this vantage, I understand Roditi's reading of the poem, because, to paraphrase Adrienne Rich, poetry
is where we put what we don't know we know.

Nancy Kricorian was raised in Watertown, Massachusetts, which has had a large Armenian community since the 1920s. With degrees from Dartmouth College and Columbia University, she is a widely published and award-winning poet whose first novel,
Zabelle, was translated into Danish, Dutch, German, and Hebrew. She lives in New
York City with her husband and two daughters.

Using Our Hands To Speak: Women's Creativity as Personal Expression

Dahlia Elsayed

My inspiration for participating in this panel began with a rug that hung in my living room when I was growing up. It was a rug that my great-grandmother made and it was revered in our house as a fine and precious thing that we were to be in awe of. We were told the story many times of how she designed and drew the rug, and how she pulled the wool and dyed it herself. I loved the rug, especially the image of my great-grandmother's process of making this beautiful work, so I was excited by the opportunity to think about it in a larger context beyond the sentimental and personal place for which it exists for me.

I kept thinking this: that my grandmother Kayane didn't have to make a rug and more importantly she didn't have to make this rug, and at the same moment I realized that she did have to make it: that the real essence for anyone actively making art is the strong commitment to creative expression, even in the most dire circumstances. Greater than the necessity of an extra rug in the house, part of the process was her need to tell a story.

Artists do this work even when they're exhausted from doing all our other work. We do it to communicate—using our hands to tell our stories visually—a three-dimensional, tactile, silent counterpart to the oral and written narrative traditions. What makes this form of expression different, and perhaps one reason why it seems more absent alongside the others, is that these objects almost always had a dual role as a functional household object as well. They were the rugs, pillowcases and aprons that families used everyday.

This kind of women's work faced such obstacles. These objects rarely left the private feminine sphere of the home out into any public setting. Although cherished, these kinds of works weren't taken as seriously, because so much of it was personal to family histories and often served a real household purpose. At best, the work my great-grandmother did would be considered primitive or folk art, or labeled as craft, which is used too often for women working with traditional materials, or perhaps it would get the dismissive label of being decorative. These old-school, male-establishment classifications don't give these works, primarily women's work, the same sort of weight as male counterparts. In her memoir Arab writer Leila Ahmed compared the education she received at a women's college and what she learned from the women in her home. What was being taught around the table—stories of lives, politics, nature—were not taken as seriously until the same lessons were put in the academic tradition of men, at the university, where it somehow seems more valuable. She wrote that it is "the difference between cooking for the family and cooking as a chef: the same activity masculanized becomes a profession and worthy of self-esteem, honor and remuneration."

The very nature as functional objects lead these art objects to get worn, discarded, destroyed or lost. They were slept on, walked on or washed until they became worn and were then used to cover the madzoon. An object too worn for a madzoon cover was made into potholders. These things have had long and useful lives and often never left the house. The art and artist remain anonymous, kept silent in the feminine sphere of the home.

Traditionally, and still today in many Mid- and Near-East cultures, the realm of feminine creative expression begins and remains in the home, with methods associated with women: rugmaking, sewing, embroidery and weaving. These were not the media men were using out in the public sphere. But is the act very different? Women were using materials most accessible to them to document their world. The stories the material told was based on what the women saw around them: marriages, birth, deaths and quite often, the outside world.

Women artists today have been expanding the definition of art, helping these works to be seen differently, in the bigger picture of women's expression. Many contemporary women artists purposely use these traditional women's mediums, sometimes in a very non-traditional way, to help push the boundaries of those categories, like the Irish artist Mary Kelly. Her well known work called "Post Partum Document," an extensive and detailed collection of material relating to a mother and her newborn, framed feeding schedules, diapers and daily activities. Full of minutiae and details, it caused an uproar when it was shown in a London gallery. It shocked everyone that she could find aesthetic value and creative expression in something so ordinary and mundane as what she fed the baby. All the criticism about whether the work was worthy of being shown in a gallery had a "stinky" subtext that this kind of work should remain where it always has, in the home.

Specific to Armenians, keeping these pieces with us has been an even greater challenge because of all the moving around. In the case of my family and many others, because of relocations not only from city to city, but also between countries and continents, things got left behind in the moves. My great-grandmother's rug, during a period of intense Arab nationalism, was rolled up and hidden in the chimney. Years later when my mother was going to America, the family so feared that the rug would be confiscated by Egyptian authorities that it was sent by ship to relatives in Australia. Luckily, the rug eventually made its way to New York. These kinds of unstable situations make this kind of work harder to document but also more compelling because the journey becomes part of our story. As a people with such a large diasporan population it's hard to keep our family stories intact. These objects become the holders and tellers of personal histories. The rug certainly functioned this way in my household. I never knew my great-grandmother, but she was alive to me, as was her story and her passion because of this object.

She came from the town of Agn, and she left for Egypt with her husband in 1913. She brought her loom with her. She was illiterate. In Egypt her husband died and she was left with two daughters in a foreign culture. She made this rug in 1919, a transitional time in Armenian history and the brief period of independence. I think of how alienated and homesick she must have felt, how silent in this other place with this other language. It makes the act of making the rug all the more moving to me.

In looking at it, it's good to start at the bottom, like she did. There are traditional colors and patterns on the border. Just above there is the text that reads "Vokhchooyn Kez Hayastan" which translates as "Life to You, Armenia," a sentiment so full of longing that it never fails to give me goosebumps every time I read it. Above the lettering is dark green laurel and then the image of Mayr Hayastan, seated and looking regal. Above her head is Mt. Ararat, with the sun rising symbolizing the bright future of Armenia, and above that are the flags of the Eshkanootyuns with their crests. In the border along the top of the rug is my most favorite detail, which tells us where she was when she made it: a small woven picture of the Sphinx and the Great Pyramids.

I toured the Armenian Folk Museum while visting Armenia before, and I saw some great works. One was a beautiful weaving of Mayr Hayastan, from 1901, sitting among all these colorful blocks or bricks at her feet, each with the name of an Armenian city. She is lamenting over the broken state of her Hayrenik. I was so happy to see it as another example of where women's traditional work dealt with subject matter that expanded beyond the domestic. There it was, perfectly placed alongside silk embroidered pillowcases made for a bride and groom on their wedding night.

These pieces are an archaeology of women's daily lives. The ongoing documentation of everyday occurrences is the link between the kind of work my great-grandmother did and the work I am doing today, both a tradition of expression that speaks visually. Even though the materials are different and the work serves a different purpose, the expression still comes from the same place the need to visually record, to document your presence in the world around you and to keep a record of the events in your view.

For me it started as an act that was totally personal and not to be shared with people. I used to write and draw a lot and my fourth grade teacher, Mrs. Kalemkerian, gave me a gift of a journal that was lined on one side and blank on the other—the perfect format for both languages I was seeking fluency in. (It is not at all lost on me that this invitation for self-expression was given to me by an Armenian woman.)

This combination of visual and text is what I still do today, in the illustrated journals that I keep, which developed into a small series of Artist's Books, and now into paintings. My paintings are in diptych format, two panels side by side that still recall the feeling of an open book. The text and images tell the stories of time and place, like a mapping of my surroundings— personal, but with all kinds of the outside world seeping in, not unlike the subject matter of women generations ago.

Although my work ends up in public spaces quite different from my great-grandmother's work, the origins of the work still come from the same place—from a story that needs to be told to ourselves and to others. Stories through the process of telling help us define ourselves as women, as artists, as families, and as a culture.

Dahlia Elsayed is a painter and a writer. Her work, which combines text and visual elements, has been published in literary magazines and exhibited nationally. She has received many awards, including a New Jersey State Council on the Arts Fellowship, and was an artist in residence at the Edward Albee Foundation. She lives and works in New Jersey.

Seen & Unseen: Fragments from a Diasporan Filmmaker

Tina M. Bastajian

As an Armenian-American filmmaker I explore language, culture, memory, identity, displacement and the relationship between these themes. I find my material within various hybrid and exilic subjects: Armenians, women, voices and experiences, which reside in the gaps or edges of dominant culture, history and memory. This idea of finding a place, between the margins, on the peripheries, inspires both my narrative and visual strategies.

Theoretically my work reflects film/media scholar Hamid Naficy's concept of the "accented style" of exilic and diasporic cinema which he asserts is: "driven by its own limitations, that is—smallness, imperfection, amateurishness and lack of cinematic gloss. It is also driven by the style's textual richness and narrative inventiveness that is, its critical juxtaposition of audiovisual and narrative elements, discontinuity and fragmentation, multifocality and multilinguality, self-reflexivity and autobiographical inscription, epistolarity, claustrophobic textuality and spatiality, and resistance to closure." (Naficy 1999)

The title of my film, *Jagadakeer...between the Near and East,* is an Armenian term meaning fate or literally what is written on one's forehead. *Jagadakeer* explores ancestral memory, nostalgia, displacement, absence, and reconnection using the Armenian Genocide as a point of reference and visual/aural backdrop. I sought to capture or frame the elusive "visuals and fetishes of homeland and the past" (Naficy 2001) by creating stylized tableaus with exaggerated costumes, color and movement layered with real and imagined sites. Envisioning form and content as intertwined components, I used dislocation and the presence of absence for the film's structure.

Shuttling backward and forward across frames was a means to demystify or interrupt the iconic and canonized Armenian homeland narrative I have experienced as a member of the diaspora. *Jagadakeer* begins in the middle, not explaining or offering the viewer precise information about the culture or Genocide. The presumption is that the audience will not know much, and this is where I find my material—in this absence. Throughout my process I sought ways to understand and connect the fragments, and used recurring but disparate narratives that are interrupted and staggered, continually forcing the viewer to the edge of knowing the locale or how to locate themselves. These starts and stops, like memory itself, evoke a sense of homeland, a lost and enigmatic landscape.

In cinema, the frame is always arriving, and like a nomad, it is temporary and fluid. Computer non-linear editing technology made it possible for me to push the experimental, non-linear style I work within even further by allowing me to more densely layer visual and aural material as a means to create the cacophonic complexities of my own diasporic experience. This non-linear structure also provided a way to question mythical Armenian culture as it weaves the distinct tapestry that has become our lives, and voices—heard and unheard, seen and unseen. A marking of my accented cinematic style—is the use of language in my films. In *Jagadakeer*, I use Armenian, Turkish, English and Arabic to highlight shifting and multiple identities. I use the texture of voices, intonations, and residues of overheard and imagined conversations to evoke personal and collective memory. The collision and collage of these dislocated linguistic realities create for the viewer—like the exiled—another realm of impossible space to paradoxically inhabit.

I also use subtitles, text over the image, in all my work. The subtitles illustrate the act of translation, as well as provide another means to create an unsettling and constant sense of separation, distance, displacement, and longing for a shared identity between the viewer and the subject in the film. This breach between the viewer and the filmic subject is the extreme opposite of Hollywood cinema, where identification with the filmic subject is the cornerstone.

We as Armenians inhabit many identities, borrowing, mimicking and carrying languages like packages as we pass through many cultural terrains, moving from place to place. The use of multiple languages portrays the fluid and jarring, the haphazard and poetic transitions/translations of my diasporic travel, articulating my own longing and nostalgia for a language to call my own.

My video, *Pinched Cheeks and Slurs in a Language that Avoids Her*, based upon an actual childhood experience, uses language as a point or site to challenge racial innuendo. The video is shot facing a mirror reflecting an image of a stately black woman sitting at a table holding a demitasse cup. This image is layered with overheard slurs in Armenian about the woman. Behind the woman a girl skips back and forth, coming in and out of view. As the girl disappears out of the frame we hear a voice-over of a young girl questioning her belonging to a culture and language both familiar and alien as they are inherited, borrowed, mimicked and essentially woven into her being.

The central placement of the woman is not arbitrary. In the video an African-Armenian woman is placed strategically in the center as the dominant subject in the frame—a position quite opposite to what her position would be within Armenian social culture. I chose to "place" the other voices off-screen, as a present but secondary soundtrack. I wanted the questioning of the woman's presence and the racial slurs to be just barely audible so the focus would remain intently on the woman's voice and presence, as she begins to speak in flawless Armenian, translating the fortune revealed in the cup's leftover coffee grinds. It is a perceived outsider who reveals the secrets and wisdom of the coffee sediment to the young witness. Although the cup and coffee provide an "authentic" cultural sign by which the viewer can locate the woman within, the woman's skin color causes her to be "read" as an outsider. This contradiction thwarts an accurate or comfortable reading for the viewers and forces viewers to reflect on their own expectations.

I use the ritual of the cup, reading between the coffee sediment and white porcelain—an act of translation—to illustrate how we see others by reading signs and images. From my experience, the magic of the cup has always been a site where mystery and the telling of the past, present and future coexist and unfold. Through a medium, usually an aunt, grandmother, or elder woman figure, the enchantment and poetics flow from the cup, to the reader and then on to the drinker. The reading of the coffee cup explores ideas that are not usually verbalized in everyday language and/or conversation. The wisdom of the cup is revealed as it allows the narrator to tell real and imagined stories and to dream, as we do in cinema.

The ritual around the coffee cup can be understood as another way of looking at the self. The images in the grinds resemble a psychological self-portrait or imprint. Similarly, just as the coffee cup reading can be seen as self-exploration or portrayal, the mirror can be seen as a metaphor for self-knowledge or self-reflection. My use of a mirror—the entire video is the reflection in the mirror of the events—provided a way of "turning the mirror around, making the mirror the mediator between being seen and seeing oneself." (Lippard, 1990)

Pinched Cheeks explores the idea of what or who makes up the ideal or recognizable and authentic Armenian subject. John Durham Peters writes in his essay, "Exile Nomadism, and Diaspora," "Diaspora suggests real or imagined relationships among scattered fellows, whose sense of community is sustained by forms of communication and contact such as kinship, pilgrimage, trade, travel and shared culture (language, ritual, etc.)." (Peters, 1999) Certainly, Armenians have an extensive history of blending into unfamiliar or even unwelcome surroundings as they traversed into new terrain. From my earliest recollection, I've understood that cultures and languages mix and move, as people shift and travel. I indeed believed in networks among neighbors near and far. I've had an instinctual awareness and understanding of diaspora, even if I only longed for or invented these imagined relationships and networks.

Many Armenian audiences are shocked by the woman's fluency, and question her Armenianness. The possibility for the two identities (Black/African and Armenian) to exist at the same time seems to them implausible and displaced. Some Armenian audiences may accept this notion of mixed race, but I'd like to point out, that in the Armenian language there is not an appropriate term for such a hybrid existence. The Armenian word, *odar*, meaning other, foreigner, or non-Armenian seems to be the only term. Yet the idea of *odar* is almost always a negative connotation, resorting to an "us" verses "them" paradigm. The irony is that one can be both Armenian and *odar* or other at the same time.

Interestingly, Armenian stories, true, false, invented, longed for and denied, are seen as odar even among other minority cultural settings. They do not always neatly fit into the categories prescribed in ethnically bracketed programming. And the ethnic label often can exclude work from more widely seen programs, which are perhaps thematic, but not necessarily contingent on labels and nationalistic parochialism.

This gathering in Yerevan has provided us an opportunity to hear a variety of Armenian voices that are emerging into the larger globalized, social framework of culture, cinema, and art. Personally, I hope to provide to this "increasingly globalized world, where cultural differences are either marginalized or rendered invisible,"(Melkonian, 2000) a variety of dialectic work that lets us place, reframe and reposition ourselves as we demonstrate the richness that blurs, shifts and unites Armenian experiences and culture.

Works cited:

Lippard, Lucy R. 1990. *Mixed Blessings: New Art in a Multicultural America.* New York: Pantheon Books.

Melkonian, Neery. 2000. Written in a letter of support for *Jagadakeer.*

Naficy, Hamid. 1999. "Between Rocks and Hard Places: The Intersistial Mode of Production in Exilic Cinema." In *Home, Exile, Homeland: Film, Media and the Politics of Place. Essay.* New York: Routledge.

Naficy, Hamid. 2001. *An Accented Cinema: Exilic and Diasporic Filmmaking.* Princeton: Princeton Univ. Press

Peters, John Durham. 1999. "Exile, Nomadism and Diaspora: The Stakes of Mobility in the Western Canon." In *Home, Exile, Homeland: Film, Media and the Politics of Place. Essay.* New York: Routledge.

Tina M. Bastajian, a film/video artist and film producer, currently works as a Media Arts Technician at the Los Angeles Museum of Contemporary Art. She has produced several films which have been shown worldwide at many film festivals and form part of several university collections. A graduate of San Francisco State University, she has received many awards and honors.

My Journey as an Armenian-American Artist

Mary Melikian Haynes

Early Childhood

I was born in Worcester, Massachusetts to parents who were Genocide survivors and was baptized in the first Armenian church in America. When I was two years of age, we moved to Providence, Rhode Island where my father worked as a photographer. One year later I was blessed with a brother.

My interest in art began at the age of four. Much to my parents' concern, I preferred drawing and painting to playing outdoors. When people would visit, I would overhear stories of the struggles regarding genocide and survival; therefore, I became very sensitive not only to the arts but issues of human rights as well.

In another section of this article it will be revealed how these two passions unlocked a sad family secret.

Fleeing My Strict Ethnic Moorings

Although family and the Armenian community meant a great deal to me, I longed to assimilate as quickly as possible and become totally American. With this challenge, I looked for avenues into the *odar* world. At the age of twelve, I became interested in a neighborhood Christian & Missionary Alliance Church. I attended all the slide presentations of the missionaries and admired the pictures of Africa, China, and India. These images became a part of my visual memory.

In my late teens and early twenties I became attracted to a downtown Methodist church and became a president of a Wesley Foundation. We were intensely involved in addressing social issues, but it was my great joy at this time to attend the Rhode Island School of Design. Part-time work at Brown University helped to pay for my tuition since my father did not want me to have a career in art and tried to discourage these ambitions. This made me all the more determined since I saw in education the pathway to freedom and fulfillment.

Leaving Home for the City of New York

Upon receiving my Bachelor of Fine Arts Degree from the Rhode Island School of Design, I took the summer off to go to Colorado Springs to be on the work staff of InterVarsity Christian Fellowship. I stayed there until the Aspen trees turned yellow.

After several interviews in Boston and New York, I accepted the offer as Assistant Designer for Fuller Fabrics, New York, working on the Modern Masters line. Contracts with various famous painters such as Picasso, Chagall, Dufy, Miró, etc. made a wonderful entrance to New York, and subsequently my pursuit of a painting career became a reality. I managed to have some early shows and then took a teaching position that lasted three years. Although I enjoyed teaching art and taking courses at Columbia University's Teachers College, the continuing call to painting took over.

At this time I was offered a part-time position at Grand Central Moderns and worked with the late Colette Roberts, a French art critic, writer and gallery director who taught me much and said, "You are an artist and you will make it in your own way."

During these early struggles many reached out to collect my work and were helpful, including the Armenian-American community in New York.

Exhibitions of My Own Paintings

One-woman shows include the Burr Galleries, Myers Gallery, Bodley Gallery, and Dorsky Gallery in New York. Several one-woman shows took place in Boston, Dallas, Scotsdale, Washington, Fort Lauderdale, etc. as well as group shows in Palm Beach, Boca Raton, Houston, San Francisco, and Los Angeles. I have also participated in the State Department's "Art in the U.S. Embassies Program."

Museum inclusions of my work are the Worcester Museum, Mint Museum, Vassar College Museum, as well as the museums of Etchmiadzin and San Lazzaro, Venice.

There have been many reviews, interviews, and articles; among them the *New York Herald Tribune, Journal American, Arts Magazine, Art News, Pictures on Exhibit,* and *Christian Science Monitor.*

Return to Roots

In 1978, I was introduced to a widower, The Very Reverend Warren E. Haynes, who was a special Lenten preacher at St. Bartholomew's Episcopal Church in New York. We were married in 1979 and my life took on new pursuits. Now, in addition to art, there was my role as clergy-spouse. A seventh-generation Floridian, my husband became involved in all things Armenian and learned about the Armenian church and culture. I saw that a return to roots was essential as we both formed a strong bridge between the Anglican and Armenian worlds.

Life As a Journey of Faith

I think that it was my Christian beliefs that gave me the courage to leave home when it was not in our culture at that time or the acceptable thing to do. So we come full circle with the multiple layers: artist, human-rights activist, wife, stepmother and grandmother, daughter, sister, niece, and friend.

In my series "The Kharpert Paintings," I uncovered the family secret. When my father, who turned 100 this past August, saw my involvement in his past, he brought out a photograph of a maternal uncle and wrote the following disclosure on the reverse side. My uncle, Khachadour, who along with me and my father were already safe in the USA, was sent back to bring the rest of the family here. Tragically, it was 1915 and he was butchered by the Turks and my mother, younger brother, and other members of the family also perished.

After my father released this information, I realized he was carrying much anger, guilt, and other scars after never getting over this trauma. Even though he was a very young boy at that time, he must have felt some responsibility.

I do not know what lies ahead, but I believe at the Alpha and Omega I will have a paintbrush in one hand and a Bible in the other. I have kept the faith.

Mary Melikian Haynes is a graduate of the Rhode Island School of Design with a Bachelor of Fine Arts Degree. She also studied at Columbia University Teachers College. Besides being a painter, she has taught art, worked as a textile designer, and gallery assistant director. Her paintings are on exhibit in many museums and are included in the Art for U.S. Embassies Program of the State Department. She has painted a series on her parents' former city of Kharpert and her work has received favorable reviews in both general and arts publications.

Effective Leadership—Challenges and Opportunities

Shakeh Kaftarian, moderator

The Third International Conference of the Armenian International Women's Association in Yerevan presented the participants with a great opportunity to get to know each other, and become familiarized with each other's points of view, philosophy, and unique challenges. Presenters reviewed the historic records of the Armenian women in Armenia and the diaspora, and reflected on: 1) the long-term effects of the genocide; 2) domestic and social issues impacting our women; 3) issues pertaining to our women's physical, psychological, and spiritual health; 4) our women's rights and gender-specific challenges; 5) our women's role in the arts, education and business; 6) the changing model of the Armenian family and the newly evolving position of women in modern society; and 7) challenges our women face in all arenas of life, regardless of geography.

The plenary session of the final day of the Yerevan conference was devoted to an examination of the need for a strong female leadership in Armenian society, as well as the challenges and opportunities that our women face in leadership roles. The audience was repeatedly reminded of the colossal economic difficulties experienced by the Republic of Armenia, and the vulnerable position of our leader and non-leader women in this shifting socio-economic system. Several presenters highlighted the need for strong and effective leadership to help transition Armenian women through this difficult and shifting socio-economic period. Several speakers posited that women must go from traditionally accepted auxiliary positions to essential leadership roles, in order to survive, reach their full potential, and assume their rightful place in society.

In their eloquent speeches several women of power and position in the present day Republic of Armenia indicated that the need and the opportunities of the Armenian women are not congruent. It was suggested that the government and political structures of the Republic of Armenia must be modified to allow women to have access to decision-making positions. They indicated that it is only through leadership roles and active participation in public decision-making that women can fully impact their fate and the future of their children. In fact, throughout the conference it was pointed out that everywhere in the world women must exchange their spectator roles for active leadership positions—in order to be heard, accounted for, and achieve better life conditions for themselves and their children. It was agreed that it is through active presence in the political and economic arenas that women will be able to attain, maintain and expand their spheres of influence in the society.

Several presentations discussed the importance and the need for strong leadership in creating opportunities for all women in the emerging post-Soviet Armenian society, with an emphasis on the plight of the most underprivileged women. They explored the input of the newly established unions and associations, as well as the responsibility of the state and the diaspora in creating and providing sufficient economic, political and social opportunities to help raise the general living standards for the Armenian women. They examined the involvement of Armenian women in the NGO sector, and the somewhat contradictory roles dictated by tradition and modernity.

Leadership was defined by some in terms of verve, vision, well-defined values, energy, enthusiasm, action-orientation, dynamism, a sense of planning with attention to both global issues and detail, a sense of anchoring, a systematic view of challenges, collaboration with one's counterparts, flexibility, capitalization on one's strengths, as well as familiarity with one's opponents' weaknesses.

Although there is not one path to successful leadership, much can be learned from the life stories of successful leading women from different nationalities. In their in-depth interviews of successful American women Dorothy Cantor and Toni Bernay (1992) report that leading women: 1) have felt loved and special as children; 2) have been told by their parents they could do anything, including claiming the spotlight of leadership; 3) felt comfortable with their core feminine identity; and 4) in most cases they modeled after their mothers, who endorsed and validated their independence, autonomy and success.

Instead of engaging in confrontation, successful leaders negotiate. Instead of dealing in win-lose methodology, successful women are able to see and utilize the gray zones. Instead of thinking of only the present, successful leaders often think of the needs of the generations to come.

Successful women in powerful roles will tell you to: 1) take risks, but be consistently outstanding; 2) be tough, but not abrasive; 3) be ambitious, but never discouraged by unequal and unfair treatment; 4) take responsibility, but be collaborative with others; and 5) be mindful of the needs of your constituents.

Historically, women of all nationalities have been taught that helplessness and dependence is a socially acceptable way of controlling the environment. In fact, helplessness has been considered as a somewhat effective way of getting others to act on one's behalf. However, we must know that helplessness has also been defined as a lack of resourcefulness and competency. In fact helplessness will only accrue what others are willing to give charitably.

Instead of relying on charity, successful women leaders exhibit self- trust and courage, and take smart risks. They are not afraid of mistakes and setbacks—they learn from their mistakes. They listen to their impulses, as well as use their analytic resources. They demonstrate flexibility, as they shift back and forth from their traditional tracks to their professional and leadership pathways. They invest in education and training, in order to strengthen their potential. They maximally utilize their resources, in order to espouse connectedness to others. Most importantly, successful women leaders feel entitled to dreams of greatness.

Research has shown that effective leadership calls for certain characteristics that must be recognized and emulated by those who want to achieve positions of leadership (Symmes 2001). Effective leading women exhibit confidence in their skills, vision and goals, as well as modesty. They are authentic, know themselves, trust their abilities, and are truthful. They are good listeners, and operate under the assumption that they don't know everything. They are good at giving encouragement and credit to others, and have no problem showing respect towards others. They engender new ideas with old information, and are able to provide direction, challenge, support and empowerment to others. They are able to help others find their own answers as they coach and guide them through confusion and entanglement. They are able to protect their people from calamity, and are willing to expose their constituents to reality. They are driven by principles, and lead by example. They accommodate necessary changes in themselves, respond to criticism appropriately, deliver criticism respectfully, and take responsibility for their own behavior.

At the end of the fourth plenary session of the conference it seemed obvious that Armenian women must plant the seeds of leadership in their girls early in life, in order to help groom effective female decision-makers in the future. It also became apparent that Armenian women have the responsibility of collectively empowering their leading women, who are capable of designing and implementing woman-friendly paths and policies. It is only through collective wisdom and foresight that Armenian women can rise to the leadership challenges of the present, and will be able to pave the path for effective future leadership and self determination.

Works cited:

Cantor, D.W., and T. Bernay with Jean Stoess. 1992. *Women In Power.* Boston: Houghton Mifflin.

Symmes, Mary. 2001. "Women As Leaders." [February 28, 2003] http://www.poweroflearning.com/article.cfm?articleid=13242 [Ed. note: This article is no longer available online. Mary Symmes' web site is at the following address, http://www.selfinvestmentstrategies.com/]

Shakeh J. Kaftarian, Ph. D., adjunct research professor at the Uniformed Services University of Health Sciences Medical School, is research administrator at the U. S. Department of Health and Human Services. She is a founder of the Armenian American Health Association of Greater Washington and co-editor of *Empowerment Evaluation.*

Leadership: Verve, Vision, and Values

Sharyn S. Boornazian

Leadership combines thinking along a continuum, connecting through interest and collaborating to build community.

Learning is a partnership. Armenians in Armenia and the diaspora and odars are forging a growing community of trust and shared interests. The Armenian International Women's Association Conference brings us together so we can influence each other. We share assumptions, ideas, laughter, food, time, pain, and connections. This emerging group becomes a more responsive community through questions and conversations.

What is the relationship between learning and leadership (Gardner 1990; Boornazian 1994)? A leader develops leaders. As people work in areas of personal strength, leadership emerges. Experience, competence and confidence are frequently recognized with leadership. A relationship that works over time requires that both the organization and the individual be able to assess strengths and needs. Organizations that engage people's strengths are more likely to succeed because these behaviors engage human potential. This is a learning organization.

Leaders work within many systems—departments, ethnic identities, interest groups, face-to-face teams and cyber-space colleagues. A change to one part of the system creates change throughout the system. A leader's awareness of people's strengths within the organization can link the needs of the one with the strengths of the other.

I offer a cautionary tale. I read this story in Sara Lawrence-Lightfoot's *I've Known Rivers*. Katie Cannon, now an ordained minister in the United States, was driving a school bus in her teens for Head Start, an early childhood program. She learned that one of her charges had drowned the day before because "some white boys had called him into the lake... He couldn't swim, they knew it and they let him drown." Katie concludes, "Don't ever let anyone call you into the lake in water deeper than you can swim" (Lawrence-Lightfoot 1994, p. 71). This black child at five did not understand the system of white privilege and racism in the sixties. Cannon warns black women trying to survive in a white male-dominated institution, "You can't let them call you to swim in deep water... You take it where you can swim" (Lawrence-Lightfoot 1994, p. 71). We need to know the systems we function within, both the opportunities and the challenges.

Many women leaders are attracted to organizations in need of saving, according to Judith A. Sturnick, former leader for the American Council of Education: Women Leaders in Higher Education and former President of The Union Institute and University (Sturnick 1998). Assuming leadership in a troubled organization, potential deep-water, increases the chances for failure and burnout. The female leader may believe the organization's difficulties are due to "her" leadership.

Related to the attraction of organizations at risk is neglecting professional development (Boornazian 1994). Women burdened with extraordinary internal responsibility tend to neglect external exposure, career development, reflection and mentoring others.

Many of the systems we operate within—medical, judicial, educational, penal, religious, environmental, governmental—originated from men. Charlotte Bunch, author of *Passionate poli-*

tics: Essays, 1968-1986: Feminist Theory in Action, is frequently quoted, "You can't just add women and stir" (Minnich 1990, p. 27). If women's perspectives were not used in the creation of these systems, how do we modify them to be more inclusive?

At the 2000 annual meeting for the Women's Educational and Industrial Union in Boston, Renee Loth, an editor for *The Boston Globe,* spoke about the need to change physical and cultural infrastructure (Loth 2000). Advised by her high school guidance counselor not to enter the man's world of journalism, Renee, a journalist, asked this question—"Is it better for women to adopt and accept male professions or go to the more traditional women's roles?" Loth indicated that a critical mass of women in journalism gained the power and influence to address issues such as domestic violence.

Anna Julia Cooper earned her doctorate from the Sorbonne at 65 years of age. Her book, *A Voice from the South* published in 1892, captures a modern view of racism and sexism in Western Civilization:

> It is not the intelligent woman vs. the ignorant woman, not the white woman vs. the black, the brown, and the red—it is not even the cause of women vs. man. Nay, 'tis woman's strongest vindication for speaking the world needs to hear her voice...The world has had to limp along with the wobbling gait and one-sided hesitancy of a man with one eye. Suddenly the bandage is removed from the other eye and the body is filled with light. It sees a circle where before it saw a segment. The darkened eye restored, every member rejoices with it. (Minnich 1990)

"A society is patriarchal to the degree that it is male-dominated, male-identified, and male-centered" (Johnson 1997), states Allan Johnson, author of *The Gender Knot.* What happens to women and minorities in patriarchal systems? They tend to assume positions and postures dependent on the players and the environment.

Leaders make judgments. Often the thinking is dichoto-mous—right or wrong, positive or negative, success or failure. This either/or mental framework creates tension and eliminates potential strategies.

A family in crisis, a government with few women in the ranks can employ systems thinking (Segre 1996). Families and gov-ernments operate within many systems. The following example focuses on a family. What are the strengths and needs of this family? Is it the ability to stay together under one roof? Ask the family, "What do you have going for you?" Love of a parent, traditions of mutual support, a balance of talent—one who orga-nizes, another who forages—are family strengths. Ask the fam-ily, "What are your needs?" Lack of dependable health care, sporadic work, the need to stay connected. A family system with knowledge of its strengths and needs can more readily identify resources.

Often educators, social workers and medical personnel en-ter a family system as expert to provide answers and resources. However, once the intervention is done, the "expert" leaves and the system returns over time to the previous condition. Family members who identify their own strengths and needs become a resource for sustained change.

As a leader, I try to reframe either/or thinking and consider the strengths and needs of a situation. What additional resources are needed? What is the relationship between and among the systems? The drive of Armenian women to make a difference in their families, communities and organizations is a tremendous resource for constructive change. How does learning together create opportunities for personal growth and collective power?

Behaviors effective "for me, for you, and for them" are more likely to be sustained and incorporated into how we go about the business of our lives (Pursley, Boornazian et al. 1999). Greater effectiveness comes from our ability to provide a pull rather than a push (Ury 1993). Influence is more compelling with pull. Here is an illustration. Two people stand face-to-face with each other and keep the palms of their hands in contact with the partner's palms at all times. A push triggers a pushback. When a partner steps back and back with the other person still maintaining palm contact, a pulling action happens. What was the direction when the partner moved backwards or away? Who set the direction? Which action—pushing or pulling—took less energy, less resistance?

Individual needs and strengths paired with the strengths and needs of an organization create a stronger partnership. I advocate leadership through pulling. Pushing frequently emerges from judgment; pulling from shared interest. Stakeholders present the strengths and the needs of an idea and anticipate reactions to moving forward; this process builds consensus and creates partnerships. This insight strengthens the thinking, thereby increasing the likelihood of commitment and sustained action.

We live within systems. Our awareness of these systems ranges from acute sensitivity to obliviousness. By gaining another worldview, we witness other challenges and opportunities. Look at the total system, understand implications, consider the context of behavior—these are the elements to work collaboratively for systemic change.

Systems thinking and community collaboration are building blocks for community development. Armenian women live in social, political, economic and organizational systems. Leaders assess and negotiate within these systems. Too often leaders use a framework of dichotomous thinking and "one-upsmanship" rather than a framework of strengths and needs. Ongoing needs assessment in a university, a rural business, or non-profit human service organization provides a baseline for dialogue and action. Leadership development provides opportunity to become more articulate about attributes—strengths as well as needs.

Leadership training builds a support network; creates opportunities for further education; and lends support for community advocacy. Successful learning networks engage non-profit agencies, academic communities and political organizations.

Leaders transfer learning from one context to another. They model shared decision-making. Leaders begin with respect for the individual, relying on the power of intrinsic motivation and release the joy of learning. These leadership values embody respect, cooperation, collaboration, synthesis, and inclusiveness. These relationships build community. Leaders have verve, create a vision, and acknowledge the power of shared values.

Works cited:

Boornazian, S. S. 1994. *Prior Learning Assessment Using Story: Academic Access for Underserved Populations.* Cincinnati, Ohio: The Union Institute and University.

Gardner, J. 1990. *On Leadership.* New York: The Free Press.

Johnson, A. G. 1997. *The Gender Knot: Unraveling our Patriarchal Legacy.* Philadelphia: Temple University Press.

Lawrence-Lightfoot, S. 1994. *I've Known Rivers: Lives of Loss and Liberation.* New York: Penguin Books.

Loth, R. 2000. Keynote Address. Annual Meeting for Women's Education and Industrial Union, Boston, Massachusetts.

Minnich, E. K. 1990. *Transforming Knowledge.* Philadelphia: Temple University Press.

Pursley, L., S. Boornazian, et al. 1999. "Promises and Perils of Participatory Evaluation Research: Lessons from a Non-traditional Education Organization." Paper presented at conference. American Evaluation Association, Orlando, Florida.

Segre, J. 1996. "Family and Community Systems." Paper presented at Cambridge College Board of Trustees Meeting, Cambridge, Massachusetts.

Sturnick, J. A. 1998. "Challenges Facing Women Leaders in Higher Education." Address given at meeting of the American Council of Education: Women Leaders in Higher Education, Massachusetts College of Art, Boston, Massachusetts.

Ury, W. 1993. *Getting Past NO: Negotiating Your Way From Confrontation to Cooperation.* New York: Bantam Books.

Sharyn S. Boornazian, Ph. D., a graduate of Northeastern University and The Union Institute, is a former dean and director for learning and assessment. Her work in adult learning, assessment, community partnerships, leadership, portfolio development, and teacher training spans thirty years. She is currently Certification Officer at Lesley University in Cambridge, Massachusetts.

CLOSING REMARKS

Women and Policy

Hranoush Hakobyan

Ten years ago, closing the 20th century, Armenia adopted a Declaration of Independence and took the path of democracy to establish itself as a state. The foundation of a sovereign state was laid in the form of a democratic, legal, and social state. A presidential system of governance and three forms of power—legislative, executive, and judicial—were established. To build a civil society, the party monopoly was brought to an end and laws protecting speech and conscience, freedom of the press, and religious and non-governmental organizations were adopted. Later, the Republic of Armenia's Constitution was adopted. The essential pre-condition for transition to a market economy was privatization of land and enterprises.

Although radical reforms are underway in Armenia, there are still serious obstacles to development. The transition to new social relations has been accompanied by emerging new evils, like poverty, unemployment and polarization of society. The worsening social situation significantly affects women.

Women in Armenia have great potential to contribute to the development of their country. Through decades the United Nations Organization has focused on women's issues, held conferences and made decisions in this regard. So, let's touch upon some aspects of women's issues and sketch the impact of the transition on women in Armenia.

Participation of Women in the Decision Making Process.

First of all, women must participate in the decision-making process at the highest levels. In the preceding seventy years the number of women in parliament, in state governance and other systems was planned in advance. Due to the democratization process in Armenia, many values were adjusted and women running for election faced various difficulties. The quantity of women in the last three parliaments did not exceed 3 percent.

The fact that women are under-represented in governmental and political structures obviously affects the democratization process in Armenia. In recent years seven women have been assigned to the posts of vice-ministers and heads of administration. The situation is quite different in the judicial branch; over 33 percent of judges are women. A relatively large number of women is observed in the Ministries of Defense and Internal Affairs, as well as among lawyers. There is de jure equality of rights for men and women, but there is de facto polarization of their rights. However, women have found diverse possibilities and different ways to utilize their potential. They have established more than 50 women's NGOs.

To enhance women's participation in the decision-making process it is necessary:

a.   To provide equal access for women to involvement in governmental structures and to full-fledged participation in decision-making process.

b.   To strengthen the structural mechanisms of gender equality.

Women's Rights are Human Rights.

The National Constitution safeguards fundamental human rights and freedoms in Armenia. In the second chapter (Articles 14-42), for example, Article 15 stipulates that everyone has equal rights, freedoms and obligations regardless of sex and other characteristics. To talk about women's rights as separate from those of men discriminates against and, I'd say, insults women. When we say, "human rights," women's rights are included.

Armenia acceded to numerous UN documents including its ratification of the "Convention on Elimination of All Forms of Discrimination Against Women" (1979), which states that the concept of "discrimination against women" means any differentiation, exception or restriction based on gender characteristics.

Women's rights are human rights. It follows that:

a.   The law should protect human rights, including women's rights.

b.   Legislation should treat genders equally.

Women and Economy, Women and Poverty.

Today poverty is considered the main factor hindering social development in Armenia. Poverty affects mostly women and children, as they are the most vulnerable group of the population. Employment has also undergone structural shifts. Though women comprise 60 percent of those with higher education, they account for 72 percent of the officially registered unemployed. Due to changes in rôles, in most Armenian families women have become the breadwinners and providers of the means of support for the family.

The economic policy should stipulate the following points:

a.   Eliminate discrimination against women by employers.

b.   Take measures to provide training and employment for women and to create adequate working conditions for them.

c.   Implement programs targeting the reduction of poverty taking into account gender issues.

Women and Education.

Over centuries every Armenian, living anywhere, under any circumstances, has faithfully fulfilled the duty of building a house, church and school. Even in the desert of Der Zor Armenian women taught their children the Armenian alphabet, tracing the letters on the sand. Profound respect towards knowledge and educational aspirations haven't decreased, in spite of deteriorating socio-economic conditions. The cherished dream of every parent is the education of children.

It is interesting that over 60 percent of students at institutions of higher education are girls. The schools, unfortunately, face numerous challenges.

The foundation of education policy should be:

a. Providing equal opportunities for and equal access to education and training for women.

b. Condemnation and abolition of illiteracy among women.

Women and Health.

The health of women is the main prerequisite for the health of the entire population, and especially for sustaining the gene pool. The protection of mothers' and children's health is ensured by the state and the system is based on providing public health care services. Women's health care programs are rarely implemented in rural areas. Due to migration the number of sexually transmitted diseases has increased.

I must state one more fact, which has emerged in the recent years and which is also alarming. It is the problem of smoking. According to surveys, Armenia unfortunately leads European countries in this regard. Another deplorable fact is that about 30 percent of smokers are women. A "Struggle Against Smoking" program should be launched in Armenia.

In health policy it is imperative:

a. To provide necessary medical care and access to medical services for women.

b. To broaden prophylactic programs for mothers' and children's health care and to conduct women's health awareness campaigns.

Women and Ecology.

Environmental issues have no borders. Today, progressive thinkers across the globe are concerned with environmental problems. That's why, in developing international policy, great attention is paid to the connection between women's harmonious development and environmental problems. Unfortunately, during the energy crisis we witnessed a new environmental disaster, that of deforestation.

Another environmental disaster threatens Lake Sevan. The water of Sevan was shortsightedly wasted, upsetting the ecological balance of the lake. In recent years the level of the Lake Sevan has decreased by twenty meters; it seriously endangers the fauna and flora of the lake. It is obvious that Armenian land cannot exist without Lake Sevan.

Women and the Mass Media.

Article twenty-four of the Constitution stipulates that every citizen in the Republic of Armenia has freedom of speech. The law, "On the Mass Media," does not allow censorship.

It is of interest, that 80 percent of informational materials are written and edited by women. There are many qualified and experienced women in journalism, including female editors-in-chief of newspapers and producers of television programs in Armenia. Periodicals are published covering women's and family issues. Some daily newspapers have assigned a separate page titled, "Stories about Women." There are radio programs dedicated to women's issues. It is not a secret that the media plays a significant rôle in influencing and shaping public opinion and in raising public awareness of legal issues and legal culture.

In this sphere it is necessary:

a. To broaden the information field by increasing the number of printed publications and radio and television programs relating to women.

b. To shape legal culture through mass media.

Violence Against Women.

The Constitution of the Republic of Armenia prohibits any form of violence. According to surveys, domestic violence is the most common form of violence in Armenia, caused by family disagreements and disputes.

Sad to say, there is a women's prison in Armenia, where there are eighty-four women sentenced to imprisonment for having committed various crimes.

It is necessary to implement programs on raising women's awareness of their rights, on providing juridical support and psychological services for women.

To sustain Armenian traditions and to eradicate violence it is imperative:

a.   To investigate the causes and consequences of violations against women and girls.

b.   To open psychological and juridical centers to provide rehabilitation of women and girls subjected to violence.

Women and Peace.

The world is disturbed by wars and conflicts. The disagreements and bloodshed mostly affect women and children. Closing the century we became the witnesses of genocide once again. The Armenian people were shaken by the events in Sumgait, Azerbaijan. Women and children were tortured and killed only because they were Armenian. And all that happened as the world looked on. More than a half-million Armenians were deported. They lost their homes and property and became refugees. An attempt was made to suppress and stifle the Armenian's national liberation movement and struggle for self-determination. The Artsakh war involved women, too. They not only shouldered the difficulties of war but also fought against the enemy. Alas, 14 of them lost their lives. There is an old saying, "If you want to live in peace, you must always be ready for war." Our women want to live in peace. They want to enter the 21st century with expectations of new perspectives and horizons.

So, it is necessary:

a.   To ensure women's long-term involvement in peace-building processes.

b. To welcome all means of peaceful settlement of conflicts, to encourage every endeavor aimed at resolving the problem of Artsakh and to maintain stability and security in that region.

c. To provide assistance for and protect the rights of refugee women.

Conclusion

The subject "Women and Policy" is a complicated one. It has a centuries-old history and will exist for centuries. Well-developed, mature and real democracy exists in countries where men and women enjoy equal rights—where women are not dismissed from their posts, where women are not discharged from their jobs, where women are not harassed, and where women's rights are not violated. The noticeable changes and enhanced social and political activities of women inspire me with optimism that in the twenty-first century women will become a decisive factor in politics.

Works Cited:

United Nations General Assembly (1979). Convention on the Elimination of All Forms of Discrimination against Women. World Wide Web: United Nations. [October 29, 2003] http://www.un.org/womenwatch/daw/cedaw/econvention.htm